A Door of
Hope

LOLA MATTISON

PAGE PUBLISHING, INC.
Conneaut Lake, PA

First originally published by Page Publishing 2020

ISBN 978-1-64701-746-0 (pbk)
ISBN 978-1-64701-747-7 (digital)

Printed in the United States of America

Therefore, behold, I will allure her, Will bring her into the wilderness, and speak comfort to her. I will give her her vineyards from there, And the Valley of Achor (trouble) as a door of hope; She shall sing there, as in the days of her youth, as in the day when she came up from the land of Egypt.

—Hosea 2:14–15

Mother's Day

Lord, why do You cast off my life? Why do You hide Your face from me?

—Psalm 88:14

It's Mother's Day. I have locked myself into the stall of the women's washroom. The place stinks of stale beer and cigarettes, a miasma of nauseating smells. The church meets here in this nightclub on Sunday mornings; it's a strange amalgam of darkness and light—a place where dawn breaks in once a week. But today, Mother's Day, I can't see it. The walls of this washroom are a flimsy barrier against the congregation outside, which is singing praises to the God who, I feel, has forgotten me.

I lean my head against the partition and the tears fall, and with them my imagination conjures a toddler in overalls I will never see, I will never hold, I will never kiss. The most painful part of this is not my loss, but that I am married to a good man who will never be a father because he chose me, a barren and fruitless woman. To look at a future closed to him and know it is my fault—my deficiency that has brought him to this—is unbearable. With that thought, the sobs begin to choke me; a constricting mass of despair escapes, and I know I will soon be howling, and I don't care. And then fiery rage consumes me. I hit and kick the plywood partition. The old familiar cry escapes my lips: "It's not fair!"

"God! Where are You?"

CHAPTER 1

October 1972

"For My thoughts are not your thoughts, Nor are your ways My ways," says the LORD. "For as the heavens are higher than the earth, So are My ways higher than your ways, And My thoughts than your thoughts."

—Isaiah 55:8–9

I stepped out of the claw-foot tub onto the linoleum. I had hoped the hot bath would have calmed the cramping, but if anything, it was worse. Still dripping and naked, I reached toward the old-fashioned free-standing metal cabinet for a towel. The blood pounded in my ears, an ocean surf, a darkening swirl. My reaching hands grasped the cabinet shelves, and the floor reached up and slammed me. How did I come to be here on the wet linoleum, with razor blades and Mr. Bubble powder and towels strewn across my bare belly?

Worse, my mother knelt beside me, saying "Don't move!" Teenage humiliation at being seen in the nude—by my mother!— was quenched by the understanding that I needed help. I had some-how pulled the metal storage cabinet over onto my body.

I was fifteen years old, a sophomore at Central High. I was no stranger to pain during my monthly cycle, but I had never fainted before. And I was shivering uncontrollably. I could hear, from what seemed a long distance, my mother's voice. "You're burning up! What a mess. Let's get this off you!"

I would spend the next three weeks at Asbury Hospital in Salina, Kansas, steadily growing more ill and confounding the family doctor in charge of my care. I was fairly sheltered. I had never had a pelvic exam or even a urine test, and I was humiliated by the exams now being conducted. This was 1972, with fewer diagnostic tools available. The constant bleeding I was experiencing limited the doctor's ability to really discern what was happening, and so I stayed in the hospital in increasing pain and with a high fever. I had more fainting spells and began to not care whether I lived or died.

My mother was committed to her job in Ft. Riley, Kansas, as a new employee and had not yet earned the leave time that would have enabled her to stay at the hospital with me. My friends from school and my boyfriend, Donnie, visited often, but as I grew weaker and the fever continued to escalate, I was less able to appreciate their concern.

I had a roommate—a girl who had been injured in an auto accident and had been recovering from multiple injuries. I was embarrassed by her witness to my helplessness. The bleeding continued, and often the bed linens had to be changed because of the mess. I couldn't get up, necessitating the staff to care for me while occupying the bed. They were required to measure the waste I produced, which further embarrassed me. The hospital smell, the hospital routines, and the humiliating exams were difficult for a young teenager to endure.

I could look out the window next to my bed, but the view was of a row of gargoyles on the Masonic building across the street. Day after day passed with those demonic faces leering at me. The clear liquid diet of tea, broth, and Jell-O three times a day for three weeks became unbearable, and I stopped eating.

The family doctor called in a gynecologist, necessitating more mortifying exams. I was profoundly embarrassed by this. Shamed. I felt surely something had to be wrong with allowing these middle-aged men to look at parts of me that even I had not seen.

A massive infection was raging in my pelvis. The gynecologist decided to use antibiotics and a drainage tube in an attempt to control it. I was given anesthetic, and the tube was inserted while I was unconscious. The treatment began to work. The fever finally subsided, and I began to recover.

I had missed weeks of my sophomore year of high school. When I returned to Central High, I was behind in every class. I was only able to tolerate a half-day schedule before my weakened body tired. Years would pass before the full extent of the damage and an explanation for what had happened to me were revealed.

Meanwhile, my mother had come to terms with the relationship I had with Donnie, whom I met at school eight months earlier, in March. My mother had reservations about her fifteen-year-old daughter's romantic attachment to a young seventeen-year-old man. However, Donnie faithfully visited me and supported me during my illness. In Mama's eyes, he had passed some sort of mom test. In her words, "He grew on me."

CHAPTER 2

March 1972

> Enlarge the place of your tent, stretch your tent
> curtains wide, do not hold back; lengthen your
> cords, strengthen your stakes. For you will spread
> out to the right and to the left: your descendants
> will dispossess nations and settle in their desolate
> cities.
>
> —Isaiah 54:2–3

Jan turned in her seat and looked at me over the classroom typewriter. "He goes to my church. I've known him and his family forever. His name is Donnie Mattison."

"What does he look like?" I asked.

"He's got blond hair." And then, the *piece de resistance*: "He has a cool car."

"A car? How old is he?"

"He's a junior."

"And he wants to meet me?"

"Yes. I know where he and his friends hang out in the hallway before class. I can show him to you."

"Okay."

Jan and I checked the time, assuring the typing class wouldn't start for another ten minutes, and we left the room. The Central High typing room was located in a hallway at right angles with the main hallway. At the hallway intersection, Jan flattened herself against the wall and peeked around the corner to her right. "There he is. He's leaning against the wall by the stairs and wearing a blue shirt."

I cautiously hugged the wall and looked around the corner, right into the face of a smiling boy whose laughing eyes revealed he had been aware of me the whole time. He lifted his hand, pointed at me, and winked. Red-faced, I squealed and jumped back. "He saw me! He saw me!" Jan, laughing, hustled us back to typing class.

Donnie called me at home that evening. "I got your number from Jan Gunnison. Would you like to go out with me Friday? Maybe we could go to a movie." My heart was pounding. "Let me go ask if it's okay first," I said. "Hold on."

Mom was reading in bed. I said, "Can I go to the movies Friday with a boy from school? Please?" My mom looked at me over the top of her book and began the questions. "How do you know him? How old is he?" And then the words that showed me I was home free: "You have to be home by ten."

He pulled into the driveway in his green Chevy Malibu at six thirty. He opened the car door for me. It was, indeed, a cool car.

He told me that he had three brothers, that he was the third of four boys. I laughed, as I was the third of four girls. An omen! He told me that his parents were not cool, and I agreed that my mom wasn't cool either, as evidenced by her taste in music. The eight-track tape player attached to the dash of his car was playing Three Dog Night, a band that was definitely cool. He leaned his head back against the headrest and looked over at me. I noticed he had a small parenthesis near his upper lip, revealed when he smiled. Something about that caused my heart to flip.

We talked about ourselves. I realized he was a senior, not a junior, as I had told my mom. That would be a problem. But I knew it was too late. I was smitten.

We were both students at Salina Central. I was a freshman and fourteen years old. I was finally settling into life in a big city, which Salina was in my mind. I had been raised in Delphos, about forty miles from Salina. Delphos was a place kids could play outside with neighborhood friends, walk to school, and leave home on a summer morning with only an admonition to be back when the streetlights came on. My sisters and I were in 4-H and regularly attended Sunday school. Our grandmother lived in Delphos. This was small-town life, and I had been a small-town child.

However, the move to Salina came at a juncture in my life between child and teenager. In Delphos, I had had the same friends all my life. The school was small. All the teachers and neighbors knew my family and knew who to call when I painted the neighbor's garage with tar or locked my sister in the toolshed.

In Salina, life was much different. My two older sisters had left home for college and did not move to Salina with us. My mom had brought us there so she could attend Brown-Mackie business college as a way to get herself free of government assistance. We would no longer be able to count on her being home during the day. My ten-year-old sister and I had to get ourselves ready for and walk to separate schools while she wasn't there. I, as the older sister, took on necessary chores like cooking breakfast and dinner. Life revolved around school and family.

Meeting Donnie opened a new world to me.

Donnie took me to his church, where I met his mom and dad, Kenny and Waunita Mattison. He was slightly embarrassed by their wholehearted commitment to Christ. He warned me that his dad liked to proselytize. In 1972, the wave of revival that had begun sweeping the country had swept into Kansas. Donnie's mom and dad had been swept up with it. I wasn't put off by that. I had, as a child, encountered Jesus personally at Bible school, and He had tenderly brought me through a difficult childhood. I was comforted by the knowledge that this boy had a faith heritage, though it was not yet personal for him.

Donnie graduated that spring of 1972, a young graduate at seventeen years old. We dated through the summer, spending much time with his friends and cousins. He worked for his dad on the farm, which kept him very busy, but we managed to see each other on Saturday nights, and we traded off going to church either at his parents' church or mine. We went to drive-in movies. We dragged the main street in his car, listening to music. He took me to a steak house, where I ate a steak for the first time. He always seemed to have pocket money, a novelty to me, coming as I did from a financially restricted background. I thought Donnie was rich.

Donnie's dad and mom had stretched their tent walls to enfold me, as they had for many, many others. On their farm, cousins and friends of Donnie and his brothers were always present. They were put to work, they were fed, they were housed, and they were expected to participate in morning devotions. And when I visited their house, I was put to work, too, helping his mother, Waunita, at harvest and at haying time. I helped make sandwiches and fill water jugs. I steered the Massey tractor while the boys picked up and stacked hay bales onto trailers. I learned about chickens and milking and stacking firewood. I rode the ponies and swam in the river. It was a raucous and boisterous family culture, so different than mine had been.

By the time I started my sophomore year in fall of 1972, my goals had begun to revolve around Donnie—until illness changed the trajectory of my life.

CHAPTER 3

Pivotal Years

Will you not revive us again, that your people
may rejoice in you?

—Psalm 85:6

The seventies were both personally and culturally pivotal for us. During the early seventies, the World Trade Center, the tallest buildings in the world, opened. Inflation hit 11 percent, impacting income for everyone. A fuel shortage caused a federal law to be passed, lowering the interstate highway speed limit to fifty-five miles per hour in order to save fuel. Women's rights groups dominated public discourse and led to the January 1973 Supreme Court decision to call abortion a constitutional right. The war in Vietnam had claimed the lives of people we knew. The war was despised, and the soldiers fighting it were disrespected. Donnie had cousins who were serving there, and his older brother, Dale, had joined the Navy because his low draft number would have required him to serve in the Army. The drug culture was emerging, promising a new spiritual pathway, as were eastern religions like Buddhism and Hinduism. Music reflected this culture. Artists such as the Beatles openly espoused spirituality through drugs. During this national upheaval, however, God was introducing a ground swell of His own: The Jesus Movement.

Teens and young adults across America were being impacted by a move of the Holy Spirit upon our nation which birthed new music, new teachers, and new study groups. Christian coffee houses and home churches sprang up. Evangelists such as David Wilkerson in New York City and Arthur Blessitt of Los Angeles were catalysts for a wave of longing for God and for a real and personal relationship with Him. Many mainstream churches did not know how to deal with the influx of unconventional new believers, and some condemned them. Teenagers with guitars, Bibles, and crosses around their necks gathered in public places, speaking of a Jesus Who was personal, desired repentance, and offered new life to everyone.

On the national front, Christian filmmakers impacted the culture with films like *The Cross and the Switchblade* and movies about the expected return of Jesus, such as *A Thief in the Night*.

College campuses were becoming crucibles of change through ministries such as Bill Bright's Campus Crusade for Christ. My own two older sisters, Lori and Bonnie, were impacted in their campus groups. They both prayed for their sisters at home, myself and Judy, and for our mother.

Salina, Kansas, was not left out. Salina experienced revival too. Donnie's dad, Kenny, was one of several businessmen who prayerfully bought a house located near Kansas Wesleyan University as a base of operations for a young evangelist named David Baker. The house came to be called the Solid Rock. The Rock was a gathering place for itinerant music groups, for traveling evangelists and teachers, and for local teens hungry for a personal, genuine relationship with the Living God.

Donnie began to feel the convicting power of God calling him to salvation. His friends were coming to repentance like dominoes—his brother Marvin, his best and childhood friend, Gary Wilson. Though I had known Jesus as a child, Donnie's talk about his pull toward repentance appalled me. I knew that God is a jealous God and that He would not share Donnie's heart of hearts with a rebellious and selfish girl. I did not want our relationship to change. I wanted to go my own way, not God's way, and so I argued against all the Jesus freaks. I threw their tracts back at them and cursed them. I laughed at them. I ostracized them. These Christians were a growing influence in my high school at the same time that the drug culture and loosening sexual mores were also influencing it. It was us against them.

One day after work, Donnie returned to his family home and no one was there, yet the cars were there and food was cooking on the stove. He immediately thought his saved parents and brother had been snatched away by the biblical rapture and he had been left behind. He ran through the house calling for his parents and brother. Just as he was beginning to truly panic, his mom and dad, driven by a neighbor, came home. This experience genuinely put "the fear of God" into him.

Donnie's brother Dale was discharged from the Navy in the winter of 1972 to 1973. While he was in the Navy, he, like many service men during that time, began using drugs readily available in Vietnam and in the Philippines where Dale was stationed. He came back to Salina and moved into a house with one of Donnie's friends, Curtis Everett. Dale and Curtis divided their days between working and getting high.

On a Sunday in May 1973, at the end of my sophomore year in high school, Donnie and I were at his parents' house when the door opened and his brother Marvin (the Jesus freak whom we avoided at all times) walked in the door, announcing, "Guess who got saved today?"

Behind Marvin in the doorway was Curtis Everett, who had been Donnie's good friend in grade school and junior high. Curtis's face was transformed from the strung-out, dead-eyed face of a drug-addled teen. This face was nearly shining, a joyful face, a face at peace.

Donnie took one look at that face and looked down, away from the evidence of the power of God. I watched him turn his attention back to the paperwork in front of him with unseeing eyes. He looked up at me, seated near him at the big farm table. "We need to go," he said, waiting for my assenting nod. Then he announced, "We are just leaving."

Donnie and I practically flew to his car and began the one-eighth-mile drive between the house and the main road. Curtis's face held such peace and joy. My spirit responded to that joy—the spirit of the nine-year-old child at Bible school, the longing and homesick spirit of one who missed being near Jesus. My heart cried, "I miss You! I miss You, Jesus!" But I looked away from Donnie's face, not daring to show him the hunger I was feeling.

Halfway down the lane, he stopped the car. "I want to go back," he said. "I want what they have." I knew he was asking me to do this with him. By this time, it was clear to us both that this was a life-changing decision. If we jumped into this, it meant everything was on the line, including our relationship. Time seemed to slow down as we stared at each other, trembling on the edge. And I nodded. "Let's go back."

We walked back into the kitchen just minutes later, though it felt like much longer. Marvin and Curtis were at the kitchen table. Marvin looked up at his brother. "What are you doing back already?" he asked.

Donnie answered, "I want to be saved."

CHAPTER 4

Happily Ever After

Those who trust in themselves are fools.
—Proverbs 28:26b

What a headstrong, dreamy girl I was. My final years of high school had two points of focus: serving God and preparing to be married. How my mother tried to convince me to wait! How convinced I was that happy ever after was our divine right. How superior I felt to people whose love was less than ours. Everyone who cautioned us was, I thought, simply lacking in faith.

I worked after school at a nursing home, and most of my paychecks went to the wedding fund. Extracurricular activities were not football games or debate team but working and attending church and the Solid Rock. I was committed to my new church. My behavior at school had changed to an astonishing degree between my sophomore and junior years because of Jesus. Even my teachers were surprised at my new resolve to excel in my schoolwork. I joined the growing group of Jesus people. I saw my high school as an evangelistic field more than a stepping-stone to the rest of my life.

Meanwhile, I didn't look much past the idea of being married. I saved money and planned a wedding. Donnie continued to live with his mom and dad and work for his dad on the farm, though the farm economy was sliding.

We were married on August 2, 1975. I had been eighteen less than a month. Donnie was twenty. Our wedding was simple and inexpensive. My mother made my dress, my sister's matron of honor dress, and the dress worn by our niece, Carrie, the flower girl. Donnie's best friend, Gary Wilson, was his best man. The church was full of friends, family, and church family. We were certain our new life was blessed by God and that ours would be a perfect marriage. We would have perfect children. We would set out, as the Carpenters sang, "facing horizons that are new to us, watching the signs along the way, talking it over just the two of us; working together day by day." We had "only just begun."

Reality was a bit different.

CHAPTER 5

The Bad Years

Wine is a mocker and beer a brawler; whoever is led astray by them is not wise.

—Proverbs 20:1

The first four years of our marriage were not easy. During the seventies, the farm economy was tight, and Donnie's dad decided to get out of farming. He told his sons that he was selling the farm and gave them first opportunity to buy it. Donnie's eldest brother, Dale, was working in manufacturing and was not interested; neither was the next son, Marvin, nor the youngest, Billy. Donnie was the son that had stuck with farming, helping his dad and investing his time and income back into the business.

Donnie knew we could never afford to purchase the entire farm and the equipment we would need to continue operating it, but he did want to try. So his dad divided the farm into two pieces, selling the house and outbuildings and the surrounding farmland to a local builder with a large family. He sold the other portion to us. We signed a forty-year loan with the Farm and Home Administration. The pressure was on.

During those first years, Donnie took on the uncertainty of beginning a new business, making decisions that were difficult and beyond his experience. The potential for financial ruin was very real, and he carried it heavily. He was young, and his dad, though willing to lend a hand whenever he could, was clearly unable to do much more than that, as he was dealing with his own financial problems.

I wasn't much help. I worked in town, first as an aid in a child-care center and then as a clerk in a retail store at the local mall. I had come into the marriage as an eighteen-year-old with unrealistic expectations of my husband. We were both disappointed. I began to rely on my coworkers for companionship and entertainment, leaving my husband to the long hours he had to spend keeping the farm viable. I slowly turned away from him and from God, pursuing excitement and fun.

I am ashamed now of the decisions I made then. I was selfish, disillusioned, and angry. I saw another world through the eyes of the people I met on my job, which was much more fun than the pressure, dirt, and demands of farming. I began going out in the evenings with my coworkers to bars and discos. I started drinking and experimenting with drugs. I knew Donnie would not approve or accept this, so I lied to him. I hid the drinking as much as possible, but he wasn't fooled. He was living with a stranger. I was no longer willing to live the Christian life he had chosen. I wanted to go my own way.

This was a painful, devastating time for both of us. He was confused and reacted by trying to control me. I was angry at his attempts to make me conform and rebelled even more. I saved a few paychecks from my job at a convenience store and rented a cheap furnished apartment. I packed a few clothes and left.

I fully intended to divorce him. I justified my actions by telling myself that he was a good man. He deserved a wife that would serve God with him. By that time, I suspected, too, that I was not able to conceive. I used even this to justify my decision to leave. He should have a wife that would give him children.

Donnie's mom and dad didn't stop praying for me. They didn't gossip about me or speak ill of me. I believe that, ultimately, it was their nonjudgmental love and faithful prayers that softened my heart.

One Sunday after my shift at the convenience store, I arrived at my apartment to find Donnie waiting for me. He said, "I was thinking maybe we could take a road trip together to give us a chance to talk and decide what to do. I don't really care anymore if you come home or not, but I will help you move your things out of this dump." Frankly, I was tired of living on little to no money. Even my meals had been reduced to the leftover hot dogs at the convenience store where I was working. The apartment was squalid. I was lonely. Donnie seemed to care little whatever decision I made. Somehow, the shock that he was ambivalent about me goaded me into a tentative return.

After our road trip, I told him I would live as I pleased and he would have to accept that. He said he didn't care enough about me for it to matter. His only requirement was that I would go to church with him.

Over the next couple of years, angry and wounded as he was, he demonstrated kindness and forgiveness toward me, just as I was finding the other life I had been pursuing to be empty.

I began to see, through Donnie, that love was not the fairy tale thing I had envisioned. Real love didn't even necessarily mean you liked someone. Real love didn't retaliate or manipulate or give up.

Donnie showed me the love of God. How could I resist that?

One of the nasty consequences of my rebellion was alcoholism. I was the daughter of an alcoholic father and had a propensity for it myself. I was not a person who could just have one drink and stop.

Secrecy holds power over us. Hiding, lying, pretending to oneself and to others that there is no problem only gives the darkness a deeper reach into the soul. I did all those things: I lied, I hid, and I pretended. My life became a twisted pattern of secret drinking and public conformity. I attended church because it was easier to go than to argue with Donnie about it. I did have friends there, but I maintained a distance. I felt that the sermons often targeted me, and it was not comfortable to sit and listen while the pastor hounded me. I didn't know that this was simply the power and love of the Holy Spirit speaking to me. Like Pharaoh, I hardened my heart. My heart was my own. There was no emotional intimacy with my husband and especially none with God.

I told myself the drinking was not a problem. Now and then, when my head was in the toilet vomiting from the alcohol, I would pray the prayer of the alcoholic: "Get me out of this, God, and I will change. I promise."

Nearly every thought was about drinking. I hid alcohol around the house, and I lied about the money I spent on it. I looked for opportunities to drink, alone, when it would cause the least confrontation with Donnie.

One day, I was driving to the grocery store where I intended to buy groceries and write a check for an amount higher than the cost of the groceries so I could have cash to buy alcohol. As I drove into the parking lot, a song came on the radio. It was a new Neil Diamond song I hadn't heard before. He was singing a duet with Barbara Streisand, and the lyrics caught my attention:

> You don't bring me flowers.
> You don't sing me love songs.
> You hardly talk to me anymore
> When you come through the door
> At the end of the day.
> I remember when
> You couldn't wait to love me, used to hate to
> leave me…

The words to the song cut me. What had happened to me? How had we come to this? We had been the fairy-tale couple. We were going to be happy ever after. And here I was, lonely, addicted, and far from my Father's house and my husband, a man who was lonely and confused and trying to endure a loveless marriage. Surely this was not the life God had intended for us. Surely there had to be more.

I parked the car and laid my head on the steering wheel and cried out to God, finally honest about my condition. There is a promise in the Bible, in Jeremiah 33:3. "Call to Me, and I will answer you." I called upon Him, and He answered me. I felt His nearness there in that car, with a song of a broken marriage playing on the radio. I knew He had never left me. I knew He would give me strength to turn away from death and toward Him. I believe this moment was the beginning of the road back home.

I'm so thankful for those who prayed for me. I attribute recovery to the prayers of people who didn't give up and didn't condemn me. My mother-in-law and father-in-law, my husband, my sisters and mother, my church family. They were the hands and feet of Jesus to me. Thank God, thank God, thank God for His unfailing grace.

CHAPTER 6

Five Years In

For the time will come when you will say, "Blessed
are the childless women, the wombs that never
bore and the breasts that never nursed!"
—Luke 23:29

After our rocky start at marriage, the Holy Spirit had a lot of work to
do in us. Donnie and I had each inflicted pain on each other. Anger
was a constant undertow that frequently pulled one or both of us
under. I attribute the healing we experienced to the faithfulness of
God and the constant prayers of Donnie's mom and dad. We also
continued attending church, where the living Word of God probed
and washed us.

The Holy Spirit often uses the most unlikely things to effect
big changes in us. I was so critical of Donnie in those days. I held so
much animosity toward him, often looking for a fight. Once in the
middle of a tirade, Donnie took me by the shoulders, looked into my
eyes, and said, "I am not your enemy." His eyes were tired, resigned,
and absent of rancor. I could see he meant it. He was declaring himself to be on my team.

The Holy Spirit is also well able to speak truth to us, if we will
only listen. I remember a rant/prayer where I told God I didn't even
like my husband, much less love him. The Holy Spirit very clearly
said, "If you can't respect the man, respect his position." This was

a revelation to me. That new attempt at respecting my husband's position brought a realization of the weight he was carrying. I finally began to see the tremendous pressure he was under, both from the farm and from my rebellion. The hard shell I had constructed around my heart began to crack.

During another ranting prayer, God clearly instructed me to pray for my husband. Not the way I had been praying—"Lord, change him!"—but the instruction I was given was to thank God for him. I was to look for the good things about him and be thankful, in prayer, for those things.

An amazing change began in my heart at that point. God began transforming my anger into appreciation. It was a long process, and to this day, I must remind myself to look for and to be thankful for my husband's good qualities, though now they are much more obvious to me.

The Holy Spirit uses scripture like a scalpel to cut away the diseased portions of our minds. One day I was looking through the book of Proverbs and found this: "The wise woman builds her house, but with her own hands the foolish one tears hers down" (Prov. 14:1). I knew God had written this proverb for me. Who had been foolishly tearing down her own home more diligently than I? Whose hands had been at work dismantling what God had joined together? Mine.

I've heard it said that repentance is realizing one is going in the wrong direction and turning around. I was finally turning around. I had gone into marriage with a fairy tale idea of life happily ever after, completely unprepared for the reality I got. Being disillusioned, though, isn't always a bad thing. Who wants to live under an illusion, after all?

As we began to heal, we began to think about the next obvious step: children. Very tentatively we peeked through this new door. We took stock of each other, of what God had done in restoring our relationship, and decided it was time to be parents.

I went to see the family doctor I had seen since I was a child, the same doctor who treated me through the pelvic infection I had at the age of fifteen. I figured that he would know if I should be worried about anything hindering conception. He examined me and said there should be no problem at all. We started a campaign that involved taking my temperature, charts, and optimal days of conception.

It felt like exactly that—a campaign. A battle. Month after month, strategic planning and counting days and trying to be in the right place at the right time…it was exhausting and definitely not romantic. But at least we were in it together and looking forward to a mutually desirable victory.

Month after month passed. My body was reliable as a clock, ticking the months by with no conception, only the disappointing arrival of the monthly evidence that I was failing in the battle. During these years, I asked for prayer at every opportunity. I memorized the promises, and I read all the accounts of barren women in the Bible who were granted children.

Surely God could work His miracle for me too.

CHAPTER 7

Dr. Sebree

And he cried out, Jesus! Son of David! Have mercy on me!

—Luke 18:38

The waiting room was empty but for myself and two hugely pregnant women. The walls displayed posters of smiling babies, laughing babies, and nursing babies. The women were discussing pregnancy. I was surrounded by fertility.

Assuming I was a member of their prolific club, the women tried to include me in their conversation with welcoming nods and smiles. I turned my shoulder to them and my attention to the clipboard holding medical forms.

Dr. Sebree had been recommended to me by my sister-in-law, Terri married to Donnie's oldest brother, Dale. I hoped to get some answers from this consultation—some sort of resolution to my monthly cycle of hope and disappointment. I was relieved to find myself ushered into a room which was obviously his office rather than into an examination room. Pelvic exams were more than uncomfortable for me. They were dreadful. Having the wide desk between myself and this new doctor gave me a bit of security.

Dr. Sebree placed a yellow notepad on the desk and began asking questions about my medical history. I managed to relay the story of the infection I had suffered as a teen without too much emotion.

But when he began asking questions about our current attempts to conceive, I couldn't contain the silent tears that began falling. He handed a tissue across the desk without comment and called his nurse into the room.

"I would like to do a physical exam. I will give you a few minutes to put on a gown, and then we will see if we can gather more information." He was matter-of-fact, almost clinical, giving me space to steel myself for the exam.

So many things about pelvic exams are humiliating, from the paper gown to the cold stirrups. I was thankful for the female nurse's presence, lending a sense of normalcy. As I lay on the crackling paper cover of the table, I tried to pretend I wasn't there, even covering my eyes with my hands. I realized it was silly, but somehow I felt better not being able to see what was happening, as if covering my eyes would also cover the doctor's.

As he palpated my abdomen, he told me what he was looking for, and indeed, finding: damage from the infection. He said my uterus was prolapsed and that there was also evidence that scarring had resulted from the infection.

"How could my family doctor have told me nothing was wrong?" I wondered. This doctor has picked up problems with one exam.

Dr. Sebree left the room and waited for me to slip back into my clothes. When he returned, he said, "I would like to do a laparoscopy. This is an exam which requires two small incisions, one in the bikini line and one in the navel. I will be able to get a better look at what the extent of the damage is, and we will know what we are up against. I also want to see your medical records. Please complete this request and we will send it to the doctor and the hospital. There are many options open to us medically now. Don't give up hope."

Several weeks later, I checked into the hospital overnight for a laparoscopy. My past experience with hospital admission had been so unpleasant—the smells, the emotions, the pain. I knew it was necessary to find the source of my fertility problem, but it was unnerving.

Laparoscopy was not as routine in the 1970s as it is presently. This procedure was only, in the 1970s, being brought into more common use because of new innovations in lighting and camera instruments. I would be incised in the navel and also at the bikini line. Carbon dioxide would be pumped into my pelvis to give a better visual access to the organs. A scope would be inserted into the bikini-line incision to give Dr. Sebree a camera view. I would be under anesthetic during the procedure.

Pre-op the night before included abstaining from food and water and an enema to cleanse the bowel. The nurses administering these protocols tried to put me at ease with humor, but I wasn't amused. I found it nearly impossible to sleep. Hunger, thirst, and anxiety succeeded in keeping me awake.

In the morning, Dr. Sebree, in scrubs, met me in pre-op and went over the plan again. "We will have more information after this. Just relax, and I will talk to you again when it's over."

"Well, young lady," he said later. "I wish I had better news for you. Your pelvis is full of adhesions from the infection you had." In his matter-of-fact way, he said, "I would place your chances of conception at zero. Your fallopian tubes are too damaged. There are, however, other medical options we can discuss when and if you and your husband feel ready to discuss them, such as in vitro fertilization."

Other medical options? After the months of monitoring, charting, and now enduring surgery? I rolled over. I closed my eyes. I wept.

I dreaded seeing my husband's disappointment.

CHAPTER 8

August 1981

See to it that no one falls short of the grace of
God and that no bitter root grows up to cause
trouble and defile many.

—Hebrews 12:15

The ball was hit hard, bouncing toward me at an oblique angle. I
charged forward and to the left, slapping my glove onto the ground
and scooping up dirt. I was sluggish. The ball took a bad hop and
careened off the palm of the glove and into left field.

I knew I wasn't thinking about softball. I was thinking about
the sharp pain erupting in my abdomen. My mind was analyzing,
sorting data, lighting on the fact that I was two weeks overdue for
my cycle. I wondered if it could have anything to do with the laparoscopy I'd had. As useless as it seemed to be to my dysfunctional
reproductive ability, I had always been regular as a clock. The results
of the laparoscopy had so deflated me, I was only now realizing that
my clock was two weeks slow.

The next hitter came up and advanced the runners for the oppo-
sition team. I stamped down onto third base and made an easy tag
for the third out. *Lord, what is this? Lord Jesus, Lord Jesus, Lord Jesus.
Oh, Lord Jesus, this hurts.* A knot of fear was forming in my stomach—the kind one doesn't give words to. I trotted into the bench,
apologizing for my error with the ground ball.

"Are you okay?" Jannie, the shortstop, asked. "You look kind of pale and shaky."

"I'm not feeling right," I answered her. "I'm glad the game is over. I think I'll run over to my mom's and then on home. Sorry I wasn't playing so well today."

I picked up my glove and bat and walked toward my car. *Lord Jesus, Lord Jesus, Lord Jesus, Lord Jesus*, my mind chanted. *Help me get to my mom's.*

By the time I pulled into my mother's driveway, I knew I was bleeding. Maybe I could patch up here well enough to get home. The screen door banged open, and outran my beautiful niece, Rhiannon, my youngest sister's daughter. I stepped away from the car and knelt down, waiting for the open-armed collision. "Aunt Lola!" she squealed. I wasn't up to the usual whirling greeting today, but I held her close, holding the sturdy body, burying my face in the silky hair.

Rhiannon had been an unplanned child. My younger sister had successfully hidden her pregnancy from us for nearly seven months, amazingly. It was astounding that even our mother hadn't put it together until a couple of months before her birth. I couldn't understand why my sister hadn't told even me. Of all my sisters, I was closest to her. When I visited her in the maternity ward, my sister greeted my visit with tears. "I'm sorry. You want a baby so bad, and I have one I didn't plan for. I named her Lola Rhiannon. We will call her Rhiannon, so you won't be Big and Little Lola. Do you want to hold her?"

I took the warm swaddled bundle from my sister's arms and looked at the tiny face. A small person, named for me. "She's beautiful," I said.

Back in the present, I folded my arms around her squirming body and tuned in to her musical toddler voice; I was comforted. She was so alive and vital. *Thank You, Jesus, for this child. Thank You that she loves me.* Whatever was going on in my body, whatever the next few hours brought, this child was in my heart forever.

I carried Rhiannon into the house, hollering out to my mother, "We lost our game. I had a couple of runs and played third base. I didn't think I could make it home without using your bathroom on the way, if that's all right."

"Leave your quarter on the back of the tank," my mom replied as I headed for the bathroom. "Are you feeling okay? You don't look so good," she observed.

"Thanks a lot! Everybody's a critic!" I said acidly. "I think it's just that time of the month." I tried to suppress any other indications of the pain I was feeling. It had become sharper, and yes, there was bleeding. Maybe it was only late menses. Maybe the pain was coincidental. Still, I could feel a cold fear, and deep inside someplace I knew what was wrong. I opened the bathroom door and said, "I'll be fine till I get home. Sorry I can't stay."

My farm home was a fifteen-minute drive from my mother's house, on the northeast side of Salina. As I drove, my mind latched onto this pain, this bleeding, and I could feel the fear fluttering like wings. What did it mean? Could I be pregnant at last, finally, and in jeopardy? Tears were blurring my vision, but I could see movement in the wheat field to my right. Three deer carefully stepped onto the road ahead of me and stood there, gazing at my approaching vehicle. I slowed and stopped the car, arrested by their gentle eyes. Three does stood quietly, looking at me. Peace filled me. This was a gift from my loving Father, an assurance, a personal message that He knew me and was present. The deer gracefully stepped across the road and bounded away. Whatever was ahead, I wasn't alone.

The ER nurse sat on a rolling stool with a clipboard, making notes of the answers I gave to her questions. "When was your last period?" "Is there a chance you could be pregnant?" "Who is your doctor?" Wearily, I responded; wearily I waited for Dr. Sebree to arrive. He raised his eyebrow at learning of my overdue menses and said, "There's no chance you could be pregnant, but we should do a blood test anyway, just to be sure. I don't like this pain you are experiencing. I think we may need to do another laparoscopy. I will admit you into the hospital."

The room was private, thank goodness, with no roommate. I had a view of the rooftop from my bed. The pain and bleeding had worsened. Dr. Sebree entered the room in his white lab coat and stood at the foot of the bed. Not usually one for sentimentality, he reached over and patted my foot and said, "You're pregnant."

"You're pregnant." How I had waited to hear those words. And now I was hearing them. A baby. Motherhood. A family. "But," he continued, "the embryo has attached inside the fallopian tube. This is an ectopic pregnancy, and if we don't remove the burst tube, you will die." *What? What are you saying?* "There's an operating room available, and I'll have you prepped for surgery immediately. I'm sorry, but there's no choice." I'm pregnant. *I'm pregnant.*

Though I had phoned Donnie's beeper number, I had no way to know if he had received my summons. This was moving so fast. I signed the consent forms and then was hooked up to the IV pre-op meds that took me to unconsciousness.

Swimming back to the surface…dry mouth…nausea… Donnie's hand on mine…the voices. "Lola, Lola, can you hear me?" Then came the knowledge that the baby was gone. "I'm sorry, I'm sorry, I'm so, so sorry."

I stayed in the hospital for a couple of days. The surgery was called a salpingo-oophorectomy. Dr. Sebree had removed both fallopian tubes and one ovary. "We left one ovary and the uterus to avoid early menopause. There are hormonal consequences to removing both ovaries. You should resume your natural cycle."

Oh, wonderful, my sarcastic mind said. *I am barren but still must endure the monthly reminders.*

"Your pelvic area is extensively scarred. There were adhesions. I believe the infection you had in your teens was caused by a burst appendix," Dr. Sebree said. "It's amazing that your body still functions as well as it does." He smiled that stiff upper-lip smile. "There are other options. Great success has been made with in vitro fertilization, and you may have eggs that can be extracted from that remaining ovary. You will not, however, be able to become pregnant without help. We can discuss it later if you like."

A burst appendix. The family doctor who had treated me had made a mistake. If they had removed that appendix before it burst, I wouldn't be barren. None of the doctors involved had ever come up with a reason for the infection, though they did ask me pointed questions about sex. The family doctor had called my condition pelvic inflammatory disease and had sternly cautioned me that this was probably my fault. I had spent the next several years shamed, believing that somehow I had caused the original infection. I recalled that the hospital had lost the records of my 1972 hospital stay. I had signed a release for Dr. Sebree to be given them when we first started trying to have a family, but the hospital said someone had "checked out the records" and not returned them. Was the family doctor trying to cover up his mistake? Did he know all along how impossible pregnancy would be? How dare he advise us to keep charts, track temperature, and wage that grim campaign if he knew it was fruitless!

I was deeply, profoundly angry. I had grown up believing doctors were infallible—that if the doctor said it, it must be true. This was a betrayal.

And what about my husband? The thought of Donnie being in this situation through no fault or choice of his own was untenable. A damaged wife meant he would never father a child, at least not with me. Maybe it would be better for him if he was free to marry someone else. I hadn't exactly been an easy person to be married to in the first place. The thought of freeing him to marry a fertile wife surfaced.

I had several visitors while I was in the hospital, including my pregnant sister-in-law, Terri. She and Dale, Donnie's oldest brother, came in the evening. She was wearing a custom-made T-shirt over her pregnant belly with a picture of her husband Dale and the words *I did it*. Their baby was due within the next few weeks, and naturally the birth was the topic of conversation. I had no capacity to rejoice with them. I was resentful of this reminder that others could effortlessly bear children and my husband would never give me such a T-shirt. I would never experience birth.

I lifted bitterness into my arms and began to nurse it.

CHAPTER 9

Family Camp, Autumn 1981

Can I bring him back again? I shall go to him, but he shall not return to me.

—2 Samuel 12:23

Family camp had become an annual event for our small church, a weekend set aside from daily life. The church was comprised mostly of young families with children. Family camp was an inexpensive and intimate way for our church to get away together. The activities included Bible study, games, worship, singing, and sometimes, a talent show. Meals were shared in the camp dining hall. Often a guest teacher would be invited. This year it was Pastor Wayne Driver.

I had not wanted to go. I was in extreme emotional pain after the ectopic pregnancy and was not dealing with it well. I did not want to interact with other people, especially people who were feeling sorry for me. I did not want to interact with God. I wanted to isolate myself and feed my anger. The problem was, my husband was also hurting, and he wanted to surround himself with people who loved him. He reached out while I withdrew. His position was doubly difficult because he felt he needed to protect and nurture me after the lost baby. He hurt, too, but I was in too much emotional pain to be supportive.

Family camp was, obviously, a family-focused time. The learning tracks would be about personal growth, marriage, and parenting. Children and nursing babies would be there, their presence another reminder of my lost child. I did not want to go. I looked for every excuse to stay home, every excuse stymied by Donnie's gentle encouragement to go, and in the end his kindness wore me down. I went. I avoided the meetings as much as I could, and when I couldn't avoid them, I sat on the fringes of the group and closed myself off. When the Holy Spirit's presence began touching hearts, I refused to allow Him near. Traditionally, the crescendo of the weekend was the Saturday evening meeting, and I had already determined that no amount of persuasion would get me to it. But Donnie refused to fight with me. He didn't cajole. He refused to respond to my anger and tantrums, and that left me, ultimately, defenseless. I went.

Pastor Driver had been an emergency medical technician before he was a pastor. He colored his presentation with stories of patients and events from that time in his life and had saved a heartrending story for this final pivotal session.

He told of a small boy who had been burned in an accident. This child's injuries required that his bandages be changed often, which was such a painful process that the boy fought his caregivers. Wayne was a large man and strong enough to hold the child fairly still while the bandages were changed. The child was in such agony that he both feared and hated the medical personnel and was verbally abusive to them. He targeted Wayne, especially.

Pastor Driver said, "I knew it wasn't me he hated. It was the pain. Though I held him down while he struggled, my tears flowed while those bandages were removed from his devastated limbs then rebandaged. I knew the pain was necessary for healing to take place."

He went on, "Some of you here tonight have been devastated and are in pain and you are fighting against the Holy Spirit. You are angry. You are in too much pain to understand what God is doing to heal you. If that's you, come forward."

Of course it was me. As he had told the story of the burned child, my defenses were crumbling. I went forward, weeping. I joined others standing in a line, waiting for prayer. When Pastor Wayne reached me, he laid his hand on my forehead. After praying silently for a few minutes, he said, "I see a little boy in overalls. He has blond hair and brown eyes. He is in the arms of Jesus." Pastor Wayne had no idea who I was. He had never met me before. He didn't know that a few short weeks ago, the only child that I would ever conceive had been surgically removed to save my life. He didn't know that the lost child my mind saw was a boy in overalls. God had spoken a word of knowledge to this man—information he could not have possibly known. This was personal. This was a look into my heart of hearts, a place I hadn't shown to anyone. No one knew about the overalls. No one.

When Pastor Driver spoke that word of knowledge, my church family surrounded me and Donnie with tears and embraces. They had been all too aware of the anguish we had been through. Many of them had been in prayer for us. This word of knowledge was for them too.

This single word of knowledge gave us all permission to grieve together without fear. Donnie could reveal the depth of his own grief, and our church family could express their sorrow with us.

The kindness of God, the understanding that He was there in the pain and confusion, overwhelmed me. I wasn't alone. I was loved and I was known. Additionally, I could see the genuine love my church had for us. "When you walk through the waters, I will be there."

The ice encasing my heart began to melt.

CHAPTER 10

1982
Options

"Simon, son of John, do you love me more than
these?"

—John 21:15

The world around us was insultingly fertile. Donnie's brothers were
fathering children. My coworkers were having babies. New babies
were being born into the young families at my church. Most difficult
to accept was encountering unmarried women who bore children,
sometimes to several different fathers, not caring for them properly
and often supporting them via public assistance.

The people close to us knew our situation and tended to stop
their discussions of pregnancy and child-rearing when we entered a
room. Well-meaning friends asked questions about foster care and
adoption. My youngest sister even offered to be a surrogate mother
for me.

Meanwhile Donnie and I went about our daily lives, getting
up and going to work every day. I taught Sunday school and built
relationships with the children around me. My niece, Rhiannon,
especially was a joy to me. We watched our family and friends in the
trenches of parenthood and consoled ourselves by traveling, telling
ourselves we were blessed to have a lifestyle our parenting friends

couldn't have. I indulged myself and hired someone to clean our home. I spent whatever I wanted on clothes. We bought furniture and went to the movies and ate out. The days passed.

I worked for the Kansas Department of Rehabilitation Services and, therefore, had access to information about adoption and foster care. A coworker, who had adopted a son through the foster system, was a personal resource. I began to write letters, make phone calls, and explore overseas adoption. Catholic charities preferred to place children with Catholic parents—parents whose income was greater than ours. The overseas agencies required up to ten thousand dollars in application fees, nonreturnable, with no guarantee that a child would be available. These agencies also had minimum income requirements. Farming was just not a stable enough profession—the fluctuations that came with weather and prices didn't give us a steady amount of money. Fostering seemed a too-painful alternative. Donnie's cousin Larry and his wife, Linda, were foster parents. We had seen the children come and go through their household. The idea of having a child in our home and then having that child taken away seemed a devastating scenario.

Even as I began to investigate it, Donnie became more hardened to the idea of adoption. He emphatically stated, "If I can't have my own, I don't want one." His response was to put his head down and go forward, howbeit with a crusty, self-protective layer to guard his wounded heart. As he once told me, men are ostriches. They put their heads in the sand and pretend all is well.

As for me, I began to wonder if God was protecting me from being a terrible mother. After all, my past included struggles with alcohol and rebellion. I had had experience as a child with an overwhelmed single mom who sometimes took out her frustration on me physically. Maybe God knew I was emotionally unable to handle it. We began to accept the idea that we would not be parents, though I was still tormented by the knowledge that I was the reason my husband would never be a father.

I developed coping strategies. I deflected the concerned attempts of friends to question me with humor. I answered, "When are you going to have a baby?" with "Have you found any on sale?" or "Who needs a baby, I have a dog!" Then I would change the subject. I avoided the baby section at the department stores, even going so far as to use a different entrance. As for the multitude of baby showers I was invited to, I declined, sending a card of congratulations and a gift with someone else.

But Holy Spirit, kind and tenacious as He is, began to speak to me about forgiveness. I understood the bitterness I held toward that doctor who misdiagnosed my infection must be released if I was to be free. The Holy Spirit insisted that I stop resenting the mothers around me for their motherhood, and He gently led me toward real deep affection for the kids I taught in Sunday school. I believe this was the beginning of a lifelong commitment to other peoples' children. A wonderful side effect of this was that the children prayed for me. If you want to see God move, just watch what happens when a child prays in faith.

One Sunday morning, my church congregation was singing

Lord, You are more precious than silver
Lord, You are more costly than gold;
Lord, You are more beautiful than diamonds,
and nothing I desire compares with You.

As I joined in the song, I could feel the Holy Spirit asking, *Is this true?* What do you love more than Me? Immediately new lyrics sprang to my mind, and I hesitated to sing them, realizing this was a foundational desire that God wanted me to yield to Him.

Lord, You are more precious than daughters
Lord, You are more costly than sons
Lord, You are more beautiful than children
And nothing I desire compares with You.

"Can you sing this to Me, dear one? Can you relinquish even this to Me? Am I enough for you?" As I began to sing the new lyrics, I knew something deep in me that was profoundly injured began to heal. *Yes, Lord. You are enough.*

Donnie and Lola, May, 1974

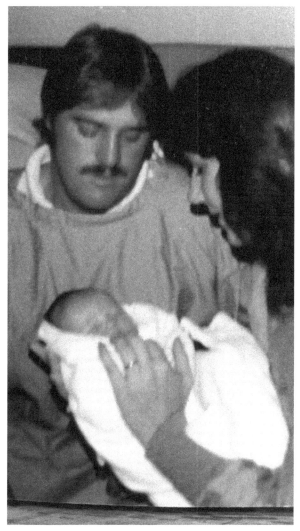

Desiree, the baby we lost 10-6-84

Waiting to meet Micah 7-24-85

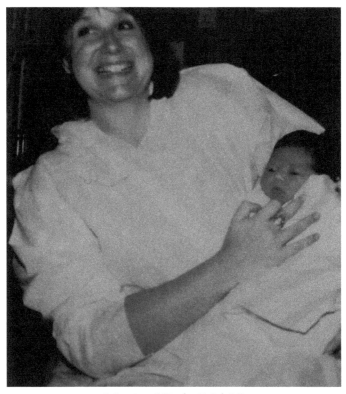

Meeting Micah, 7-24-85

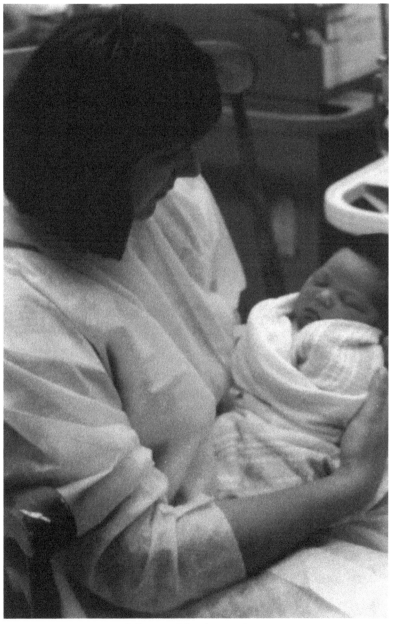

Meeting Micah, 7-24-85

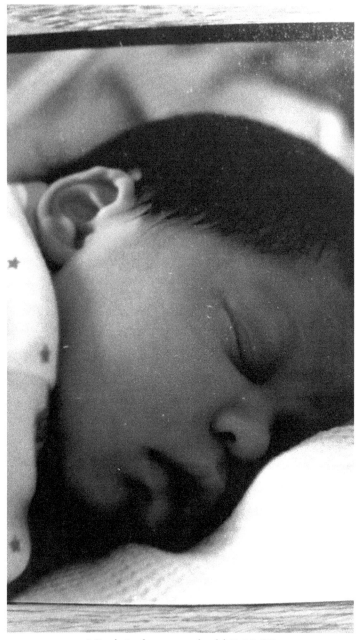

Micah Joel, one week old 7-30-85

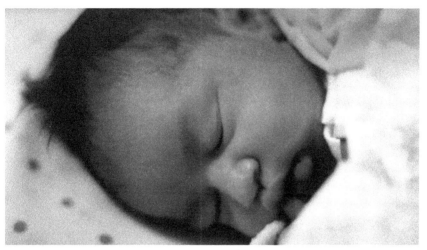

Meeting Rosie, 4-12-89

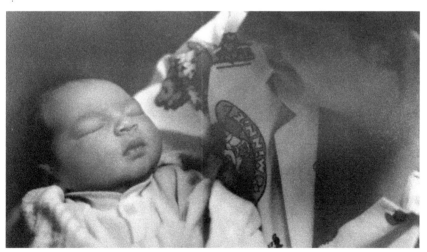

Rosie, Micah's answered prayer, 4-12-89

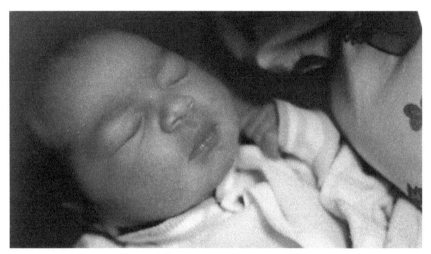

Gloria Rose, 4-12-89

Micah, age 5, and Gloria, age 2, brother and sister, 1991

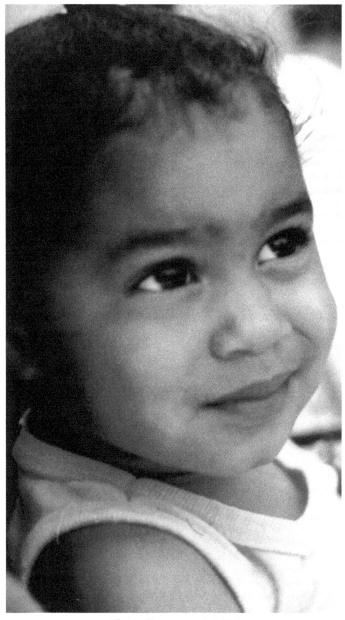

Gloria Rose, age 3 1992

Micah Joel, age 6, 1992

Micah and Gloria, grown, July 4, 2013

CHAPTER 11

Jason

He made known to us the mystery of his will according to his good pleasure, which he purposed in Christ.

—Ephesians 1:9

"Can I help you tomorrow too?" Jason looked hopefully at Donnie before clambering down the ladder. Donnie had been replacing shingles on his dad's rental house. Ten-year-old Jason had been Donnie's work buddy that August morning, but his dad had come to claim him before the heat drove them off the roof. "I don't know. We'll have to see." It was the answer no child wants to hear.

Donnie has a cousin who also farms. This cousin, Roger, had three children: Jason, Nathan, and baby Morgan. Roger's wife, Maureen, was kept busy with the kids and a husband who spent long hours away from home, so sometimes Roger would help out by taking one or more of the boys along with him to work. Donnie and Roger were always looking out for lucrative enterprises. They collected limestone landscaping rock for sale, they had a firewood business, they sometimes helped each other out with custom farming work. Jason and Nathan were used to coming along and, as they grew, lending a hand with whatever needed to be done.

Logistics is a big part of farming. Circumstances often require someone to jocky equipment or people from one place to another.

Roger and Donnie sometimes relied on each other to help with these logistic issues. Jason, at nearly eleven years old, had been entrusted with driving a tractor on fields with minimal problem areas. Jason sometimes drove the pickup between fields. Though eleven seems young to people raised in a city, it's not unusual for farm kids to learn to drive early, use tools, and to have a healthy respect for dangerous machinery. Donnie remembers being propped up behind the pickup's steering wheel in the pasture while his dad shoveled feed to the cattle from the bed. At the age of twelve, Donnie drove the tractor in the field and along the road between fields.

On August 14, 1984, Donnie woke to Jason shaking his shoulder. "Can you give my dad a ride to town?" For an instant, Donnie was disoriented, thinking Jason was there because he wanted to help finish the shingling job from the day before. What they needed was for Donnie to follow them to the corner at Old Highway 40, from where Donnie would give Roger a ride into town, and Jason would drive Roger's pickup across a bridge and about a quarter of a mile to a waiting tractor. The field in which the tractor sat was situated beside a gravel road, a straight shot from the corner.

At the corner, Roger got out of the truck and hopped in with Donnie while Jason scooted over behind the steering wheel of Roger's truck. The men waited for Jason to maneuver the truck across the bridge and watched him out of sight along the gravel road, then turned toward town.

I was at work when Donnie called me. Jason had overcorrected his steering on the gravel road and had rolled the pickup. He was thrown out of the window. The truck rolled onto him. Donnie only knew that there was spleen damage. An ambulance was taking Jason to Wichita. Roger and Maureen were following in their car. "Pray."

Jason and Nathan were special boys. Donnie had spent lots of time with them, and he loved them. This accident hit him hard. I could hear the tears in his voice as he relayed the message to me. I immediately laid my head on my desk and began to pray for Jason, for Roger, for Jason's mom, Maureen. And then the phone rang again.

"He died!" Donnie sobbed. "I can't believe it! I had a feeling as I watched him drive away. I just had a feeling!" Donnie was nearly incoherent, but I understood enough to know that this precious boy was gone.

The funeral was grim. Jason's brother and sister, his mother, his grandparents, and the extended family were uncomprehending. My own recollections of the funeral are jumbled. What I remember most was the terrible anguish.

Roger and Maureen invited the family to their beautiful farm home for the wake. Nathan, Jason's brother, still so young, didn't quite understand what had happened. He and the younger cousins saw this is an opportunity to play and made a beeline for the trampoline in the yard. We adults sat, shell-shocked, the laughter of the younger children an incongruity. My attention was arrested by the kids and their joy in being given a chance to let off steam after the long funeral service. I was glad they were too young to grasp the enormity of what had happened.

One little boy stayed inside, looking out the screen at the other children. I didn't recognize him and wondered if he was one of the kids Roger's brother and sister-in-law were fostering. He was very slight, nearly too thin.

"Hi. What's your name?" I asked.

"I'm Brian. Hey, hey, come here. I'll show you sumpthin'." He took my hand and led me across the dining room to the porch. "I'll show you sumpthin'," he repeated.

"I need to stay inside, Brian, but you can go outside if you want." Brian looked out at the other kids and then led me back to my chair.

"Hey," he said. "Hey, I'll show you sumpthin'." His brown eyes were large in his small face. He had a slight stutter, endearing in a little guy. He began to chatter to me about a toy car he had. Roger's sister-in-law, Linda, Larry's wife, noticed my interaction with Brian and sat beside me.

"I see Brian's got a new friend," she said. "Social Services called us as emergency caregivers. I don't know how long we will have him. He sure is a talkative one." Linda explained that Brian would probably be available for adoption soon.

I considered Brian, wondering that beautiful children like him were in foster care while Donnie and I wanted children so badly.

I looked over at Donnie, Roger, and Larry, standing in a tight threesome, their grief-stricken faces set. Which is worse, I wondered, to have had a son and lose him to an accident or to have no child at all?

A few weeks after the funeral, Donnie and I lay in bed talking about how hard it was to wake every morning and have grief there waiting at the end of sleep, waiting with its heavy presence at the edge of consciousness, waiting to relentlessly blanket the coming day. Donnie said he was surprised he could grieve so for a child that wasn't his. I think that's when God began to show him that it is possible to love a child he didn't father. This is how his mind began to change toward adoption.

CHAPTER 12

Desiree

The LORD gave and the LORD has taken away;
blessed be the name of the LORD.

—Job 1:21

My mother looked at me across the kitchen table, her brown eyes hopeful. "Strangely enough, this woman's name is also Lois, like mine," my mother said. "She has a seventeen-year-old daughter whose baby is due in October. No husband. A deadbeat boyfriend. Lois is encouraging her to have the baby adopted. I wondered if you and Donnie would be interested."

My mother had been heartsick for us. Never one to talk about her own struggles, especially to her children, I hadn't realized how much she was suffering too. My mother, Lois, and her coworker, Lois, each had a problem: one with a teenaged, single, pregnant daughter, and one with a barren daughter. How natural they should see the solution to both problems.

I had done enough investigating to know that a private adoption in Kansas was a straightforward process. We needed an attorney and the money to pay the bills. If this girl was willing to relinquish her baby directly to us, the adoption agencies were not necessary.

Donnie, through Jason's death, had realized how deeply he could love a child he had not fathered. When I spoke to him about the baby my mother had mentioned, he didn't reject the idea. "Maybe this is what God wants for us," he said. "Roger has a lawyer friend who sings in his barbershop quartet. Maybe we should talk to him."

Dan Boyer's office was everything one could imagine for a lawyer—leather sofa and chairs, barrister's bookcases filled with law books, a desk stacked with files. "Kansas does require a home study conducted by a licensed social worker. I can set that up for you, if you like. I will contact the birth mother to get her signature on some paperwork. When the baby is born, I will meet with her to have the documents signed, relinquishing her parental rights. You will have expenses in regard to the social worker, the hospital, and of course, my legal fees."

Donnie and I, seated together on the leather sofa across from his desk, took a moment to look at each other. Now that we were looking at a real possibility, were we ready? Would we be good parents? Is this the plan God had for us?

Donnie reached for my hand. He turned to Dan and said, "Go ahead."

Later, on the drive home, we dared to hope. We would need to paint the second bedroom. We would need baby furniture. And what about names? It was so hard to imagine that we might actually soon be parents.

Dan phoned the following week to let us know that we could expect a call from the social worker, who would inspect our home and interview us. The social worker would prepare a report which would be part of the petition to adopt.

At work, I arranged to use my accumulated vacation days as leave for the baby's homecoming. It was not the usual maternity leave plan, as I was ineligible to use any medical leave. I would only have a couple of weeks at home. I also consulted my friend Virginia, who had adopted a child through social services. Virginia told me the social worker's visit was nothing to dread. She would be asking questions about our child-rearing philosophies and checking that our income was sufficient and that our home was suitable. When the social worker came, we were ready. We had cleaned our home and painted the nursery, discussed how we would answer the inevitable questions about discipline, prayed together, and presented a united front.

She was a nun—a small wizened woman with thick glasses, wearing a habit that looked like it belonged to someone larger. She carefully laid a yellow legal pad and three pencils on our dining room table and began the questions.

We were interviewed both together and separately. We also were asked to find people who would be character references for us. These people would write letters of recommendation directly to her, and she would incorporate these into her report to the court.

While we waited for the birth, we considered what names to choose for the baby girl. We settled on Desiree, which meant "desired, longed for." For a middle name we chose Nicole. The meaning of Nicole is "victory of the people." How fitting.

I served as a state officer in my professional organization, the Kansas Association of Rehabilitation Secretaries. The first week in October was the annual convention, which was to be held in Manhattan Kansas that year, and I was attending. That Friday night, October 5, at midnight, I got a call from Donnie at the hotel that our baby girl had been born at eleven o'clock. I dressed, packed my overnight bag, and went out into the night to retrieve my car and drive home to Salina. I carefully fastened my seat belt, thinking, *I'm a mom. I have to be careful now.*

By the time I got home, it was one thirty in the morning. We tried to sleep but found ourselves wakeful. We held each other and made plans. We discussed the fears and joys all new parents face. Very early on Saturday morning, Dan phoned, letting us know we were free to visit our new baby in the Geary County Hospital in Junction City. Donnie's mom and dad wanted to come along, of course, and drove us to the hospital in their car.

We checked in with the information desk upon arrival and were directed to an open patient room on the same floor as the nursery. We were all given gowns and masks to wear. Donnie and I and his parents seated ourselves and waited for the bassinet to be wheeled in. Within minutes, she was there, the tiny bundle swaddled in a cotton blanket, the tiny face absolutely lovely. Our baby. Our Desiree.

We took turns holding and exclaiming over her perfection. Donnie's mom and dad took photos with their Polaroid, which ejected the finished grainy photographs of us in our hospital gowns. She was so tiny, so helpless. So beautiful. Though we wanted to stay longer, Donnie's mom and dad had to get back to Salina, so we said goodbye and left our baby with promises that we would be back that evening.

We went home and bought diapers, tiny onesies, and a new dress for Desiree's homecoming. We bought crib sheets and bumper pads for the borrowed crib. With Desiree's room ready, we picked up my mother and took her back to the hospital to meet her new granddaughter. She had a gift for us—a new baby book to record the accomplishments of Desiree's first year. Back at the hospital, the nurses carefully inked her tiny feet and printed the footprints in the book for us. My mother was overjoyed. She was full of advice for us, exclaiming over how perfect Desiree was. We stayed and held her. We unwrapped her to count all her fingers and toes. And then it was time to leave. Once more we tore ourselves away, watching the bassinet roll back toward the nursery. We stripped off our masks and gowns and made our way back to the car and the drive home. My mother wasn't usually one to talk about her feelings, but she was nearly giddy on the drive home. She was feeling thankful for her role in finding Desiree for us.

Dan, our attorney, told us that we would be able to bring our new baby home the next day, on Sunday afternoon. He planned to be at the hospital to get the birth mom's signature on the last document: the relinquishment papers. We would go to church and let our church family know we were finally parents, in answer to all those prayers, and then in the afternoon we would meet Dan at the hospital and bring our new daughter home at last.

Sunday dawned, a joyful morning. At church our friends rejoiced with us, asking questions about our new daughter. She was seven pounds, five ounces, twenty-one inches long, born Friday night, October 5, at 10:55 PM. She was perfect. We were naming her Desiree Nicole. We repeated the information again and again, to each inquirer, amazed at the news ourselves.

Donnie's mom and dad, again, drove us to Junction City in their car. My mom came along. We loaded the diapers, the dress, an extra outfit, and the car seat into their car and set out. Our little welcoming committee arrived in the hospital lobby expecting to be ushered up to the nursery, but the receptionist asked us to wait there. Of course, we figured, we must wait for our attorney. He had not called that morning, but that was to be expected. We had prearranged to meet him here.

We took over the lobby waiting room, chattering, the grandparents looking at the Polaroid photos. And we waited. After the first half hour passed, Donnie checked in with the desk to see if Dan had called, but he hadn't. We waited another forty-five minutes, wondering what could be keeping him. I began to feel the first tentacles of fear. I asked at the desk if the birth mother was still in the hospital, and we learned that she was. I asked if our attorney had been in earlier; they replied negatively. More waiting, but we waited quietly now, losing confidence that the plan would unfold as expected.

The phone call came a quarter of an hour later to the hospital receptionist. Donnie was summoned to the telephone, where Dan spoke to Donnie. I stood near, my cheek touching his, to hear Dan's voice over the receiver say, "I'm so, so sorry. The birth mother changed her mind." I didn't listen to the rest of the conversation at all, but instead returned to my seat in the waiting area, stunned.

Our formerly happy group was now tearful. We tried to comfort one another, but it was so overwhelming, so hard to grasp. Donnie was crying like I had never seen him cry before. We clung to one another for a while, just letting the knowledge sink in, and then we asked if we could see Desiree one more time. The hospital staff said that would not be possible. We looked at our little pile of supplies— the diapers, the clothing, the car seat—realizing we had no need of them now. I turned to Donnie and said, "We should leave these for her. The birth mother doesn't have anything for her. She didn't plan to leave here with a baby." We asked if we could take the things up to the birth mother.

When I look back at this, I'm amazed that the hospital staff allowed it. Donnie and I left the grandparents and took the supplies into the elevator, trying to get our emotions back under control. The elevator door opened into the maternity ward, and we turned toward the birth mother's room. Her door was open. She was there in bed, holding Desiree. There were two other people in the room, but I barely registered their presence. Donnie and I knocked gently and stepped into the room.

"You will need these things," I said. The faces in the room registered shock as they realized who we were, and then they, too, were crying. "We wish all the best for you and for her," I said. We piled the items just inside the door and, blinded by tears, turned to go.

Back in the elevator, both Donnie and I were crying too hard to see the floor numbers light up. We were barely aware of the car ride home. Donnie's dad managed to drive us all back, but everyone in the car was devastated.

It took a few hours to be able to function at all. At home, the phone was ringing, first with calls from well-wishers and then, as the news spread, with friends offering condolences.

I couldn't bear to go back to work the next day. I wasn't expected, anyway. Donnie's grief drove him to busyness, however. He had wheat to plant and work to take his mind off the pain.

I lay on the floor in a heap, overwhelmed, crying out to God. I had made it through all the previous painful events, but this? This was too hard. This was too, too hard. "How could You allow this? I can't bear it. I feel as if I'm dangling over a chasm, clinging to a thin thread, and it is not enough. I will be swallowed up by this. I am not strong enough. I can't bear Donnie's grief. I can't bear this yawning sorrow. You, Lord, are only a slender, fine filament, a mere thread, and this horrible pain will consume me. How dare You require me to cling to You now? This red slight thread—it is not enough! It is not enough! But Who else do I have? Who else do I have but You?"

Donnie and I gathered the rest of the items from the nursery and took them to Terri and Dale. Terri was a volunteer at Birthright, a local organization dedicated to helping mothers with unplanned pregnancies. I asked her to donate them. We visited awhile, and then I asked her if I could hold their three-month-old, Jonathan. Any mother knows that it's a very bad idea to disturb a baby that has finally fallen asleep, but Terri was not only my sister-in-law, she was my friend. She lifted his warm body into my arms and left me there in the room, in the rocking chair, to hold him. I held Jon and prayed for Desiree and her birth mother. I prayed for my grief-stricken husband. I lifted Jon's fragrant head to my face and traced his features with my finger, so gently, careful not to wake him.

Clinging to Jesus felt as insubstantial as clinging to a thread. But I had no one else. I remembered the account in the gospel of John of followers leaving Jesus after He spoke to them of eating His body and drinking His blood. Confused and appalled, they couldn't take in His strange words. Jesus turned to the twelve and asked, "Do you also want to go away?"

Peter answered, "Lord, to whom shall we go?" Like Peter, I knew that I had no place else to go.

Surely the One that held the world in His arms was holding me too.

CHAPTER 13

In Vitro Fertilization

Before I formed you in the womb I knew you...
—Jeremiah 1:5

Donnie took the crib apart and carried it down to the basement, intending to return it to Roger and Maureen when he could bear it. I closed the door of the spare bedroom and kept it closed. I placed all the Polaroid photos in Desiree's baby book and stored it away, along with the letters of consolation our friends had sent and the congratulatory cards we had received before we lost her.

I went back to work, where my coworkers quietly avoided talking about their own babies. We resumed daily life. Donnie and I tip-toed around our obvious grief, not wanting to subject each other to scraping open the wounds.

I had a scheduled appointment with Dr. Sebree for a checkup. He asked if Donnie and I would be interested in going to Kansas City and checking out in vitro fertilization, or what the media had dubbed "test-tube babies." He felt that I was physically capable of producing eggs and possibly carrying a child to term. It was a matter of being referred to the fertility experts at the Kansas University Medical Center for further consultation.

This seemed to be a way out of the dead-end road in which Donnie and I had found ourselves. We agreed to have Dr. Sebree make an appointment for us with the fertility department.

In 1985, there was no internet. There was no WebMD. IVF was a rather new procedure, the first test tube baby having been born just seven years earlier in 1978. Dr. Sebree gave us the bare bones: fertility drugs would stimulate my remaining ovary to ripen as many eggs as possible at once. These ovum would then be extracted and fertilized with Donnie's sperm in vitro, "in glass," in a test tube or petri dish. The fertilized eggs would then be transferred to my uterus, and then the chances were about 20 percent of a successful pregnancy.

It started snowing the night before we left for Kansas City for our January 1985 appointment at the KU Medical Center. We decided, just to be on the safe side, we would take Donnie's four-wheel drive Chevy truck, even though it got only eight miles to the gallon. The snow continued throughout the drive to Kansas City. We saw several accidents and stranded motorists. Ordinarily, Donnie would have stopped to help, but we had to be in Kansas City in time for our appointment.

We arrived only ten minutes late. We traversed the labyrinth of hallways with the help of signage and a few requests for direction. In the conference room, four other couples were already seated around a U-shaped table. Our names were printed on the cover of a loose-leaf binder on the table. To our right, a man stood in front of a media screen. He welcomed us, expressing surprise and relief that we were able to drive through the snow to get there.

What followed was a two-hour presentation on the protocols of IVF. The cycle for each attempt was two weeks. Each attempt cost $9,000.00. Each attempt would require at least two trips to Kansas City. Each attempt, as Dr. Sebree had already told us, had a one in five chance of success. When the question-and-answer portion of the presentation started, I asked, "What happens if several eggs are fertilized?"

"The medical team will determine how many of the fertilized eggs are viable and make a decision at that time how many will be placed in utero" came the answer.

"What happens to the nonviable embryos?" I asked.

"They are discarded."

By the time we left the medical center, the snow had accumulated several more inches. We discussed staying overnight in Kansas City, but I was due at work the next day. We decided to chance it. Rather than stopping for lunch, we ate snacks in the truck and headed back onto I-70. The snow was coming sideways, thick, obscuring vision. We were only able to drive between forty and forty-five miles per hour, and the road conditions only worsened. The radio was reporting that the Highway Patrol was closing the highway west of Salina. We decided to stop in Junction City, about fifty miles from home, and wait till morning to travel the rest of the way.

Donnie and I lay in our motel bed and discussed the in vitro presentation. We knew already that my insurance would not cover the costs of in vitro fertilization fully. We also knew that discarded embryos were discarded babies. The Bible is clear that conception is the beginning of life. Neither one of us was willing to allow our embryos to be discarded. In vitro was not an option.

The final door was closed.

We slept. We woke. We waited for the snowplows to open the highway. We went back home, and we tried to adjust to a future as a childless couple.

CHAPTER 14

The Ski Trip

And if anyone gives even a cup of cold water to one of these little ones who is My disciple, truly I tell you, that person will certainly not lose their reward.

—Matthew 10:42

"Just once more? I finally have the hang of it," I said pleadingly. I looked from face to face. Dale and Barb, the Minnesota natives, had grown up on skis and ice skates. Donnie and I, however, were new to skiing. We had put in a full day on the slopes, and they were ready for a soak in the heated pool, dinner, and deep sleep. Donnie had taken to the skis quickly. He had been slaloming along confidently for several trips down the slopes. I, however, felt that I had only just gotten the technique mastered sufficiently to relax and enjoy the downhill rush.

"How about it?" I asked.

"Okay," Dale answered. "But let's up the game and take a more difficult slope this time."

I had been content so far to stay on the easiest slope, where the children and other newbies were tumbling under the watchful eye of their instructors. With Dale and Barb there to guide us through the basics, we eschewed the paid instructors to save some money.

This March 1985 trip to Silver Creek resort in Colorado with Barb and Dale had been planned for eagerly. Donnie and I both were wearing our new ski bibs and thick gloves, and I was sporting matching parka and hat. We may not have been the best skiers, but we sure looked cool. Our friends had taken time with us, teaching us how to buckle ourselves into the strange, forward-slanting boots, how to catch the chair lift, and how to sidestep uphill wearing the awkward skis. Donnie and I had stayed on the bunny slope, while Barb and Dale cut loose with the experienced skiers. We had spent the entire day in the bright Colorado sun and snow. Now everyone was tired and ready to warm up and rest, but I wanted one more shot at skiing.

We made our way toward the lift, Dale and Barb skiing like they had been born skiing. Donnie, behind them, still an obvious learner, was moving with confidence. I was the caboose.

At the top of the slope, Dale and Barb swooped away, snow cascading off their skis. They skied circles around us. Dale, especially playful, glided closely behind and alongside, gently teasing me for my careful left-right-left-right attempts to slow down on this steeper decline. This slope was not as smooth as the one I had been practicing on. There were bumps and small crevasses to maneuver. The others stopped at the brink of one of these to wait for me to catch up so Dale and Barb could demonstrate the gentle jump that would take us over the gap. Dale and Barb each sailed over twice, just to show us how it was done. Donnie gathered speed, jumped, and tumbled but rose triumphant. Now my turn. I was at a full stop facing the crevasse. I flexed my knees to begin the push downhill. I felt a *snap!* My knee buckled. I fell.

"Get up, honey. You can do it!" Donnie called. "It's not hard at all!"

"Something's wrong with my knee," I answered as I tried to stand.

"Oh, come on. You're okay! You can't be hurt. You weren't even moving!" he answered. I could tell he was a bit frustrated with my drama, but I knew something definitely had been injured. I tried, again, to stand up. There was no pain in my knee, but there was a loose feeling, an instability, and when I put my weight on it, the knee wouldn't hold me.

Dale and Barb made their way back up the slope to me and tried holding my arms and maneuvering me downhill, but it was obvious I wasn't going to get down the mountain that way. "I'll go down to the first aid station for help," Dale said, and in seconds he was flying across the snow.

It was just like me to be the party pooper, I thought. I straightened my leg as far as the ski boots would allow. Surely this was just a weird sprain or something—it didn't even hurt! I began to feel an edge of anxiety about ruining the trip for everyone else. Donnie certainly seemed to think I was being ridiculous. Hampered by the skis, I tried again and failed to stand up.

Soon we could hear the sound of a snowmobile roaring up the mountain toward us. It carried two people and was towing a long bright orange sled. The snowmobile entered the soft powder near me but began to sink. Gunning the engine, the driver steered toward the snowpack but couldn't extricate the machine from the softer snow, and it sank deeper. I was reminded of an old *Gunsmoke* episode involving cowboys caught in quicksand.

Finally, the driver pulled a radio transmitter from the snowmobile and called for backup. A second snowmobile roared up the mountain. The first order of business was for the medics to haul me to the orange sled and strap me in. I looked up at the blue sky and thought, *Unbelievable. Not only do I injure myself, but it takes the whole first aid department to rescue me.* Immobilized in the sled, all I could see was the sky, but I could hear the sound of the snowmobile's engine powering up. The sled began to move and, as it gained speed, the wake of snow coated my face. It was a bumpy ride.

Back at the lodge, sans skis and boots, I found that I could ambulate if I held my leg slightly bent and used it more as a prop than as a moving part. Somehow, we got to our room. I felt so bad that I had caused the day to end on this sour note, I told them all to go eat and to bring back something for me later. The medics had given me an ice pack and an ace bandage. I propped pillows under my leg and sent everyone off. "Go! Don't let this ruin the trip!" The knee had begun to swell and stiffen. I was glad to just sit there in the quiet. It was a chance to pray.

The original plan for the trip was to have two days of skiing. We had spent quite a bit on lift tickets and equipment rental. None of us was willing to waste it all. I told the others I would enjoy myself just fine alone and that they should go ahead as planned and ski the second day without me.

As the day wore on, my knee continued to swell. I still thought it was probably only a sprain, so I kept walking on it. However, when I stepped down, the tibia would slide backward. It felt so loose and strange, I knew it had to be more than a sprain. Something was very, very wrong.

When he returned from the slopes, I told Donnie that I thought I should have it looked at. The last thing we wanted was more medical bills, but I was afraid I might injure it further in ignorance. A small clinic specializing in ski injuries was located, opportunely, about a half mile from our lodge. There I was x-rayed and examined by a doctor who seemed much too excited about my injury. He called two interns into the exam room and had each of them watch as he slid the tibia forward away from the femur. "This is a typical presentation of torn anterior cruciate and medial collateral ligaments," he intoned. Then he had each of the interns feel the looseness of the knee joint. I was a regular celebrity to them.

"Go see your orthopedic surgeon when you get home," he said to me. "You will need surgery."

By the time I had a consult with Dr. Kruckmeyer back in Salina, my sense of irony had kicked in. Dr. Kruckmeyer, a small bespectacled, serious man, looked at me gravely. "There will be extensive repair necessary. I will make an incision approximately eight inches long, with several layers of stitching to repair the two tears. You will be in a cast afterward and will need physical therapy to get your range of motion back. If you had been a football player, this would be a career-ending injury."

I ducked my head and asked, quietly, "But will I be able to play the piano?" I glanced sidelong at Donnie, sitting in the chair beside me. Dr. Kruckmeyer, a confused look on his face, answered, "Of course." I smiled and said, "Great! Because I can't play it now!"

After surgery, my left leg was encased in a cast from the ankle to the upper thigh, bent at a slight angle, just enough to prevent me from sleeping on my stomach. Every six weeks, I would go back to Dr. Kruckmeyer for evaluation and once to change the cast. Every six weeks, I would expect to have the cast removed, but in answer to my questions, he would always answer, "See you in six weeks."

My arms became my legs for those eight months from March to October on crutches: strong. Sleeping was difficult—the cast scratched Donnie so much we had to cover it with old panty hose. Heat and sweat were uncomfortable and smelly. I could also see the muscles in that leg were atrophying.

God used those eight months to work humility in me. I had to ask for help, nearly every day, for some necessary activity. I had to have help bathing to keep the cast dry, help opening doors, and help hauling laundry baskets upstairs; I had never been good at asking for help. I hadn't considered that refusing help from those who offered it in love was refusing a blessing for us both—that allowing yourself to be served also allows someone else to have the joy of serving.

I got a call from a lady whom I had privately categorized as needy. She was obese, financially dependent on others, and intellectually challenged. But she offered her help to me in any way I chose. She called every week or so to encourage me, sing to me, and pray with me. Oh, how humbling it was for me to see that God doesn't see others as we see them. The marginalized are often those He chooses to show His kindness.

I learned to use crutches very well. I could maneuver nearly anywhere, including on stairs and escalators. Donnie and I decided to take in a Kansas City Royals baseball game that July to celebrate my twenty-eighth birthday, which required ascending and descending the stadium steps on crutches.

We spent the night in one of Kansas City's loveliest hotels in Crown Center, the Sheraton. This was a splurge for us. This hotel had all the amenities, concierge parking, restaurants, lovely rooms. Our room was near the top of the building. Because my birthday fell on the fourth of July weekend, a fireworks display was featured at the Crown Center plaza. Donnie and I made ourselves comfortable in front of the floor-to-ceiling windows and watched fireworks explode at eye level.

Our conversation turned to our future. This was our life now. We were childless, but we would make the best of it. We would travel. We would have freedom that couples raising children didn't have. We would trust God that His plans for us were good, even if they weren't what we had hoped for. Both of us were finally where God wanted us.

Two weeks later, everything changed.

CHAPTER 15

July 23, 1985

I prayed for this child, and the LORD has granted
me what I asked of Him.

—1 Samuel 1:27

I glanced at the clock and sighed. Two more hours until quitting
time. I could probably finish typing this evaluation report if I kept
at it. I did a neck roll and adjusted the awkward metal and Velcro
brace on my left leg, which I had propped on an open desk drawer.
I wanted to wrap up this task, knowing I would be away from work
the next day for Grandpa Gawith's funeral. Grandpa died on July 22,
and the funeral was tomorrow, the twenty-fourth.

My intercom buzzed, and Claudine's voice called out, "Lola,
you have a call on line one." I finished the paragraph I was typing and
then punched the blinking button on my phone.

"This is Lola," I said as I propped the receiver between my
shoulder and head and set my fingers on the typewriter keys. I did
want to finish this report. Typing was, by now, nearly automatic. I
could transcribe without fully engaging my mind.

"Lola? This is Dr. Sebree. Do you have a moment?"

What on earth? Now I was fully engaged. I pushed my chair
away from the typewriter and reclaimed the phone receiver in my
hand. Whatever could he be calling me for?

"Sure," I answered.

"This afternoon I delivered a baby boy here at the hospital. The mother has checked herself out and has signed the papers to relinquish him to be adopted. Apparently, another couple was set for the adoption, but they have changed their minds. I thought of you and wondered if you would be interested in adopting? Before I call social services, I wanted to check with you. He is healthy. He weighed in at a little over eight pounds. He is a biracial child, with a white mother and a black father. I realize you will need to check with your husband, but I will hold off on social services if you want me to."

I took the phone away from my ear and looked at it. *Am I dreaming?* I wondered. *What did he just say?*

"No! No, don't call social services! How can I reach you? I have to check with Donnie, but please, please don't call social services!"

Dr. Sebree wasn't much of a chuckling kind of man, but he chuckled now. I quickly wrote down the phone number he gave me and promised to get right back with him. My mind began spinning out thoughts like cotton candy. First, tell Donnie.

I swung the heavy braced leg off the open desk drawer and punched an outside line on the phone, keying in Donnie's beeper number. Now to wait for him to call me back.

My whirling thoughts threatened to carry me off, so I captured them and brought them to God. "Father, is this from You? Father, is this Your plan? Please, please let it be Your plan. Father, I'm afraid. Father, I want to believe this. Father, oh Father, oh Father…"

Claudine buzzed in. "Donnie's on line one for you." As I began to explain to Donnie what Dr. Sebree had said, I had a bit of a reality check. We had to think about this biracial thing. Donnie's family might be a problem. "So what?" I said, impetuous as always. "They aren't adopting him. We are!"

"We don't want him to be hurt, do we?" Donnie asked.

"Of course not!" I replied. Into my mind came a picture of Elizabeth Joy, the baby daughter of our associate pastor and his wife. Doug and Barb were a mixed couple, and yes, they had encountered some bigots. Steve and Debbie, another couple from our church, had told me a story of being refused service in a restaurant. I realized we could face some challenges, but already rising in my heart was a fierce militant determination.

"We can deal with it if we have to," Donnie was saying. "Call Dr. Sebree back and tell him yes."

CHAPTER 16

Meeting Micah

The grace of our Lord was poured out on me
abundantly, along with the faith and love that are
in Christ Jesus.

—1 Timothy 1:14

Donnie looked at me doubtfully. "What if we see him and then it
all falls through? I don't think I can go through that again." Donnie's
words, I knew, were his way of saying he couldn't deal with his wife
falling apart like before. "Let's wait for Dan to get the legal paperwork filed or whatever he has to do and then go see the baby." I
thought, again, how our failed adoption had positioned us to move
quickly now. We had Dan, the attorney, already lined up. We knew
what legal steps were necessary, and we still had that crib. We had
also settled on a name, one we had both loved for a long while. It was
Micah, which means "who is like Jehovah," His middle name? Joel,
"Jehovah is God." It was a declaration of God's amazing intervention.
We had named him, but we hadn't told anyone yet.

Wednesday morning, I sat in a funeral parlor chair in Minneapolis,
Kansas, trying hard to keep the giddy smile from returning to my face.
Instead, I focused on Grandpa Gawith, Donnie's maternal grandfa-
ther. His wife, Beatrice, had been the chief caregiver for Grandpa in
his war with diabetes. Just in the last year, one at a time, both legs
had been amputated. I watched Grandma Gawith's face registering

sorrow and resignation. I had admired their relationship. Donnie and I played canasta with them occasionally. Grandma and I would pair up as partners against Donnie and Grandpa. Grandma could be competitive, crowing with delight when we won. I wondered if the news of a new great-grandson would lighten her heart now. *Monday's child is fair of face. Tuesday's child is full of grace, his birthday is July 23. My birthday is July 5. Two and three make five...* how my mind was dancing, sorting the facts, looking at the coincidences. *Tuesday's child is full of grace.* With that thought, the smile returned to my face.

The family met at Grandma Bea's house back in Salina in the evening for a family dinner. There were all Donnie's maternal aunts, uncles, cousins, and brothers who had traveled home for the funeral. We had told Donnie's parents and, of course, Dale and Terri. I sidled up to Terri now, bursting with it.

"Have you seen him yet?" she asked.

"No. We want to get the paperwork finished first. We are both afraid something could go wrong."

"Let's go see him now!" Terri's eyes shone with excitement. "I will have Dale watch the boys here and I will go with you. We would only be gone a few minutes. No one will even miss us."

"Without Donnie? I don't know. What if something goes wrong?"

"What if you miss this opportunity?" Her question hung there between us. I knew Donnie was gun shy, wanting some legal protection for his heart before he gave it away. My heart had already, sight unseen, been taken.

"Okay!" I hoisted myself onto my crutches, made my way across the room, and whispered my plan into Donnie's ear. He turned to me with concern. "Do you want me to come with you? I need to be here, though." I knew he was struggling, remembering the terrible pain we had experienced. "No, you can stay here, Terri will drive me. We will only be gone long enough to look through the nursery window."

Hospital visiting hours were over, but Terri and I made our slow way up to the third-floor natal wing, my crutches squeaking along the quiet hallway. At the window, we looked at the swaddled bundles lined up facing the window, but all of them had cards with names and vital statistics. Toward the back of the room, away from the observation window, another bassinet stood in the shadows, a light from the nurses' station shining on it like a beacon. Peeking out from the swaddling blanket, two bright chocolate eyes looked into mine. I know, newborns are not supposed to be able to see more than eighteen inches, but those eyes were open, and they belonged to the most beautiful baby in the hospital, and they were looking at me. "There he is! There he is!" I pointed to the bassinet.

"How do you know?" Terri asked.

"I know."

Terri was an amateur photographer. She had her thirty-five mm camera with her wherever she went. Tonight was no different. She hoisted that camera and focused on the tiny face. A nurse looked up and saw us. She opened the nursery door and reminded us that visiting hours were over. She must have seen something in my expression, because she closed the door and walked over to me. "I think that's my baby," I said, realizing as it came out how strange it sounded.

"Are you Mrs. Mattison?" she asked.

"Yes! Is that him?"

She smiled and gave my arm a squeeze. "Let's see if we can arrange a meeting." Within minutes, she and another staff nurse brought us inside the nurses' station. I could obviously not hold a baby and hold myself up on crutches at the same time, so they located a rolling office chair for me. After washing and gowning up, they pushed the bassinet up to my chair and placed the warm bundle in my arms.

The photographs Terri took that evening are priceless. Cameras required film in those days—no digital, quick selfies then, no little camera window to review the photo. One had to wait for the film to be processed and printed. Terri captured the joy of the moment—even the nurse's laughing face is in one of the pictures. There is no fear in my face, no panic. I had no time to be afraid; I had no one else's feelings to worry about. For those minutes, that tiny baby was the only person who mattered. This surprise meeting between us was a gift from the God Who Sees Me.

By the time we got back to Grandma Gawith's house, the cat was out of the bag. The rest of the family knew. Grandma Gawith took Donnie's hand and kissed him.

"You know," she said, "when one dies, another is born."

CHAPTER 17

Hurdles

I will turn their mourning into gladness; I will
give them comfort and joy instead of sorrow.
—Jeremiah 31:13

We had many preparations to make. I went to work Thursday, July
25, to make arrangements with my supervisors for vacation leave and
to allow them to hire a temporary staff person to cover my job. It was
again clear to me how God had used our failed adoption to prepare
the way for us to be ready for Micah at a moment's notice. Even the
temporary staff person had been in His plan. My sister-in-law, Terri,
stepped in. We also had an attorney, and he had all our vital information in his files. The home study was lined up. As I was thinking
about this, I realized that it had been nine months since Desiree was
born. At the very time Donnie and I were dealing with our biggest
loss, Micah was conceived. Indeed, as Genesis says, what the enemy
had meant to harm us, God had meant for good.

One huge hurdle still to be jumped was the financial situation.
The hospital required that we pay all the expenses of the birth, the
birth mother, the circumcision, and the hospital nursery before we
would be allowed to take Micah home. No payments. They wanted
the entire bill paid in full. We did not have $2,600. Sometimes I
think God likes to show off a little bit. I know He loves to surprise
us. Just as we were discussing the problem, Donnie got a call from

Chopper, a trucker from Oklahoma, asking if Donnie had enough alfalfa in small bales to fill a semitrailer. Chopper was on his way north and wanted a load to take back to Oklahoma. The amount he paid? $2,500. Cash.

Friday morning, Donnie and I were at the hospital early. It began to sink in for Donnie that this was really happening. Because Micah's birth mother was nineteen, we felt more secure that, as a legal adult, she was making a binding decision. She had also checked out of the hospital after Micah was born, so we weren't fearful that she would appear and demand to have him back. Still there was a constant reminder that this process was only beginning and that there were many things that could go wrong.

The attorney needed to meet with us, but I was determined to stay in the hospital with Micah. Donnie went without me to Dan's office. The proverbial wild horses would not drag me away.

The hospital offered a class for new moms on basic infant care. The class was in a small room, and the attendees were all new mothers in robes and slippers. And then there was me, obviously out of place. Surrounding me were young women dealing with hormones, lactation, physical rebound…and my stressors were all internal. They were worried about breastfeeding. I was worried about keeping my baby.

We watched a short film, and then a teacher lectured on basics. She went over breastfeeding at length but also discussed bottle feeding, diapering, how to care for the circumcision wound, how to clean the remaining umbilical cord, and other topics. I looked around at the company of new mothers and realized that, even though I was in street clothes, I had been born into a new demographic. Motherhood. I am a mother. This is forever.

After the class, I stood at the nursery window and gazed at Micah. The nursery staff still had his bassinet positioned on the back row. The blue card taped to the bassinet read "July 23, 8 lbs. 4 oz, 20.5 inches." No name. Did that mean anything? Was there yet another problem?

Two other women were there, one of which I knew casually. She was a social worker. "Hi, Nancy!" I greeted her. Neither of the women were wearing hospital attire, so I concluded they were visitors. Their heads were together as they exclaimed over the babies and smiled.

"Look at that one! Look at all that curly hair!" Nancy pointed at Micah.

"I want that one!" her friend said.

I turned on them and roared, "No! He's mine!" The outburst even shocked me. Nancy took a step back. My mind, contemplating legal requirements, had jumped to the conclusion that somehow in her capacity as a social worker, she was there with her friend for the same reason I was—adoption. My overreaction was embarrassing. "I'm sorry. It's just that we are here to finish the paperwork so we can take him home. We are adopting him."

Tears sprang to Nancy's eyes. "I've been praying for you. That is very good news."

Donnie was delayed at Dan's office. Kansas had a change in the adoption laws that were effective July 1. The hospital had records they would not turn over to Dan until he provided required documents to them. He could not provide the documents to the hospital without the records they were refusing to give him. It looked like a standoff. Dan negotiated a solution, and the last hurdle was cleared.

At four in the afternoon, on Friday, July 26, we brought home our three-day-old son. Within an hour, the house was full of friends and relatives who came to welcome Micah into his new family. Because of Grandpa Gawith's passing, all those relatives were still in Salina. Grandma Gawith was one of the first to hold him.

We had no baby furniture, no surface to place a baby except the center of my bed. I was still on crutches, my leg in a thigh-to-ankle brace, so I welcomed our visitors on the bed with baby Micah and all his worldly goods: hospital formula in tiny glass bottles and ten diapers. Soon the bed was piled with tiny outfits, Grandma Gawith's hand-crocheted booties, even a Cabbage Patch doll with curly hair just like Micah's.

Chris Kinny came. She and her husband Mike had one child—a daughter named Jennifer. Chris and Mike had been staunch friends to us, never wavering in their faith that God would bless our home with children. Chris told me that she and Jody Olson, another dear friend, had walked around the room that would now be Micah's nursery, praying that God would send us a child to live there. Chris and Jody had laid hands on the walls. "Father, send this couple the desire of their hearts." As Chris gazed at Micah, tears ran down her face. "God is so good," she repeated. "God is so good."

Terri was there with her camera, taking pictures of my first attempt to change a diaper. She brought our nephews, Daniel and Jonathan. Jon had turned one year old the day before, on the twenty-fifth. He sat on the bed smiling around his pacifier at his new cousin. Jon and Micah would grow up together.

Something else she brought were the baby items I had asked her to donate. There were the receiving blankets and sheets I needed to get the crib set up. She had kept them as an act of faith. Again, it was clear that God had turned our grief into joy. The framework for our new family was in place, constructed through sorrow, ready to house joy.

My sister, Bonnie, took me aside. Bonnie is a registered nurse with a second degree in early child development. Bonnie's life had been going through transition as well. Her present occupation as a geriatric nurse was not a good fit for her. She missed caring for the babies in the pediatrics unit. That day, my sister offered to care for Micah full-time when I returned to work in three weeks. How could I ask for a better solution? Someone educationally and spiritually qualified, someone with extensive experience with newborns, best of all, someone who would love him. I was overjoyed. I knew we wouldn't be able to pay her the salary she was accustomed to, but she said she could accept what we could pay.

My sisters were there, my mother, and Donnie's parents. Our house was bursting at the seams with joy. What an outpouring of support. Aunts, uncles, and cousins there to witness a day we never thought would come.

On Sunday, we dressed our tiny son up for church, but a spit-up requiring a change of clothes delayed our arrival until after the service had started. When we slipped in the back, Pastor Loren stopped in the middle of his sentence, and the congregation turned to see the baby they had prayed for make his entrance. We looked around at the faces of so many that had walked through this journey with us. So many of them had prayed in faith when our own faith was lacking. This wee child's presence was a testimony to God's faithfulness.

Micah was a celebrity, a flesh-and-blood manifestation of grace. Micah's adoption was like a pebble dropped into a pond, with ripples touching places we could not have foreseen. People we didn't even know were touched by God's goodness in sending him to us.

Donnie and I frequented Green Lantern, a convenience store on Iron and Ohio streets. The employees there passed the hat for us, presenting us with a gift for Micah. I tucked the enclosed card into his baby book with the others. I marveled at the plan unfolding before me. None of this would have been possible without first enduring the loss. *Micah, who is like Jehovah? Joel, Jehovah is God!*

Isaiah 54:1 says, "Sing, O barren woman, you who never bore a child; burst into song, shout for joy." Yes, who is like Jehovah?

CHAPTER 18

August 2, 1985

Jesus looked at them and said, "With man this is
impossible, but with God all things are possible."
—Matthew 19:26

I snugged the flannel blanket around Micah's arms and laid him on
the living room couch, pillows creating a nest in the corner. Sleeping
as only a baby can, he was undisturbed. I leaned in close, drinking
in his scent, placing a kiss on his curls. Today Micah was a week and
four days old. Today was also our tenth wedding anniversary.

I was discovering my husband. After ten years of marriage—
through "for better, for worse"—in my juvenile way I believed I
knew everything I could know about him. I was so wrong. The husband I thought I knew had turned out to be a steel creampuff. I had
never seen him so tender as he was with Micah. There was something
beautiful about those big callused hands cradling Micah's tiny body.
I felt as if my mental image of him was cracking, tiny pieces flaking
off to reveal a man I didn't realize was there.

Neither of us wanted to leave our baby that evening for an anniversary dinner. However, ten years was a milestone, especially for us.
At one point in our marriage, neither of us had expected to have a
tenth anniversary. It must be celebrated.

I was ready with paper plates and a picnic blanket spread on
the living room floor. Donnie was picking up a pizza from Scheme,

the ultimate family-operated pizza purveyors in Salina. We had no gifts, no flowers. We had no Hallmark cards. What we did have was a family.

Later, Donnie reached into the box for another slice of pizza while I leaned against the sofa. Micah was lying, wrapped and warm, on my chest. Donnie looked up at me and said, softly, "Happy anniversary." I replied with a smile. He said, "I didn't believe we could heal. I really didn't."

"Yes, it's miraculous. Happy, happy anniversary." I reached out to him, smiling into his eyes, and I thought of the scripture "Nothing is too difficult for Me."

CHAPTER 19

I Know the Plans I Have for You

What I have said, that I will bring about; what I
have planned, that I will do.

—Isaiah 46:11

"And Jesus, please give me a brown baby sister named Rosie." Micah's three-year-old face, eyes closed, was earnestly turned heavenward. "Amen. Good night, Daddy. Good night, Mama." With a yawn, Micah snuggled under his quilt and closed his eyes.

"Good night, son." Donnie and I looked at each other, wondering about this new nightly petition for a baby sister. We had explained to him that God didn't give babies to us the same way He gave them to other families. God would have to do a miracle to give him a baby sister, not to mention a brown baby sister named Rosie. Micah, however, was undeterred.

"Jesus can do it, Mama."

In my own room, I knelt and prayed. "Father, he's only a little boy, and he doesn't understand. Please don't let this be a stumbling block to his faith. He trusts You, Father, that You can do anything." I sighed. I worried that, as a brown child with white parents, he felt the burden of being different. I wondered if this prayer request reflected a desire to have a family that looked more like him. "Father, I pray You would show him how loved he is." As for the Rosie part, all I could figure was that he'd been watching *Follow That Bird*, a Sesame

Street movie in which children named Rosie and Floyd befriend Big Bird. I supposed I should be relieved that he wasn't asking for a brother named Floyd. "Abba, please don't allow his childish faith to be damaged. Show us how to explain this to him."

I knew the faith of a child was nothing to be scoffed at. After losing Desiree, the first and second graders in my Sunday school class had made cards for us, many of them containing prayers that God would give us children. In the following weeks, I assured them that, indeed, God had given me children: them. These children loved me—a profound gift—and they prayed for us. And now we were parents. I was convinced that the prayers of children are especially precious to the Father.

Our little family had settled into a routine. I was still working for the State of Kansas five days a week. My supervisors had accommodated my desire to spend more time at home and allowed me to come to work at 7:00 AM. With a half-hour lunch, I could leave at three thirty in the afternoon. Donnie did the morning duties. My sister, Bonnie, arrived at our house at around 8:00 AM and stayed with Micah until I got home.

Bonnie and Micah were great buddies. She had a gift for dealing with small children. They all loved her, but this was a special relationship. Bonnie was there for all the milestones. Her nursing experience was a godsend to me. She recognized the staph infection Micah picked up as a newborn in the hospital. She recognized the symptoms of ear infection. She worked with us through the infant formula changes as we searched for a solution to his stomach upsets. I was a tentative, new mom with no experience at all. She helped us with everything, from giving Micah his first bath to toilet training. Most importantly, I knew she prayed for us. Micah loved his Aunt Bonnie.

Micah's Daddy called him pal. Farming gave flexibility to allow them to spend time together as Donnie fed the neighbor's cattle or fired up the tractor to work the fields, little Micah falling asleep in the tractor cab. I had a willing helper to stir cookie dough, sweep, or dig in the garden. Our lives were rich, fuller, and more satisfying than I could have hoped. It never entered my mind that there could be more.

I was at work in February 1989 when the desk phone buzzed, and Claudine's voice said, "Lola, call on line two. It's Pat Neustrom." I reached for the phone receiver, thinking, *Pat Neustrom? I don't know a Pat Neustrom.*

"Hello, is this Lola Mattison?"

"Yes, how can I help you, Mr. Neustrom?"

"I have an unusual opportunity for you. Do you know Dr. Steven Sebree?"

"Of course. He is my doctor."

"Dr. Sebree has indicated to me that you and your husband may be interested in adopting a baby. I understand you already have an adopted child, a biracial child, is that correct?"

My mouth went dry. I propped my arm on the desk to stop the tremble in my hand.

"Yes, we have a three-year-old son."

"Dr. Sebree gave me your names as potential parents of a baby due in April. Would you and your husband be able to come in to my office and visit with me about it?"

"Yes, we would. May I call you back after I speak to my husband? Could you give me your phone number and a couple of options for an appointment?"

*****

Pat Neustrom was a smallish bald attorney in a power suit. He ushered us into a conference room sporting a long polished table and seated us in two chairs at one end of the table.

"I've been contacted by a colleague, an attorney in Hutchinson, who represents a woman due to deliver a child in April. Her sonogram indicates the child is a boy. The attorney is looking for an adoptive family for the child, as the couple initially lined up has decided against it. I called several attorneys and doctors for advice, and that's how I got your names from Dr. Sebree."

Donnie and I looked at each other. We had already decided we were open to listen to the attorney's proposal.

Mr. Neustrom passed a square white paper across the table to us with a figure written in black ink. "This is the amount you will need to cover your legal fees and expenses. Of course, the cost of the home study will be determined by the social worker. The mother has gestational diabetes, which should not impact the baby, but her obstetrician is requiring that she not work until the baby is born. She will have car payments, rent, and monthly bills that will need to be paid as well." Donnie and I exchanged glances again. Our experience made it abundantly clear that this mother could bring us right up to the birth and change her mind, and we would have nothing we could do about it. The previous year had been awful on the farm. Drought had decimated the wheat crop. Firewood and hay sales had kept us in groceries over the winter. How would we cover our own living expenses and take on hers too?

"The birth mother would like you to correspond with her, through my office and her attorney's office, as she wants assurances that your family would be a good fit for her child. I will give you a few minutes to discuss this, but I will need an answer soon so another couple can be located if you decide against it." With that, Pat Neustrom left the conference room.

Donnie reached for my hand, and we bowed our heads. "Father, guide us. We know that You can do anything. If this is Your will for us, please give us the provision and grace to go forward. If this is not what You want, please close the door."

If we had learned nothing else from the past, we learned that God is bigger than we are and that He can do anything. When Pat returned to the conference room, we said yes.

CHAPTER 20

Now We Wait

> In the same way, the Spirit helps us in our weakness. We do not know what we ought to pray for, but the Spirit himself intercedes for us through wordless groans. And he who searches our hearts knows the mind of the Spirit, because the Spirit intercedes for God's people in accordance with the will of God.
>
> —Romans 8:26–27

I reach into the tiny basket and draw out my cross-stitch project. The needle is already threaded with a double strand of olive-green embroidery floss. It is a small piece, the pattern sporting briar roses, a butterfly, and the words "All things work together for good to them who love *God*." The project is not only something to keep my hands and mind occupied, it is a prayer. When fear begins whispering the litany of potential roadblocks to the adoption, I reach for this fabric and needle and the words from Romans 8:28. All things.

All things work together for good. Teenage appendicitis. Inept doctors. Ectopic pregnancies, failed adoptions, death. All these things can be turned by a loving God to work together for good.

I glance at Micah, focused on plowing the living room carpet with a toy tractor, rows even and smooth through the pile. Here is a living, breathing testimony of that goodness. If God can do that, He can do anything.

The first letter I sent to Anita, the baby's birth mother, apparently was enough to convince her that we would be suitable parents for her baby. With each support check we sent through the attorney, I would include another letter. I had since learned that she had another child, a girl, who was coincidentally the same age as Micah, three and a half. Knowing that she already understood the problems of being a single parent helped me believe she was serious about going through with the adoption. I wondered if the fact that the baby was a boy motivated her. Donnie and I had chosen a name, Noah, for this child. We had not told Micah yet. It would be unbearable enough for us if something went wrong; we didn't want Micah grieving as well.

So far, God had provided income to cover Anita's bills and ours. Donnie and his dad were hired to do a demolition job on a house near the country club. This house had been built around a mobile home. The lot it was sitting on had been sold, and the new owner wanted to build a new home there. Not only were they being paid for the demolition, but they were given the mobile home to sell.

Somehow our finances were stretching to cover the need. I had notified my supervisors at work that I would need some time off in April. Terri, my sister-in-law, had been hired full-time and was unavailable, but I had been spending time each day training a temporary office assistant. The State of Kansas still restricted my adoption leave to vacation days. I would have to take leave without pay for most of the six-week period I wanted with the new baby. Still, I was thankful that Kansas provided insurance coverage for adopted children just as if they were born to us. We would need to come up with the medical expenses incurred by Anita, her hospital and gynecologist bills, but the baby's would be covered by my insurance through work.

We planned to keep the baby in our room for the first few weeks, and then move him from bassinet to crib in Micah's room. The two boys could share a room. We were having a struggle finding a social worker with a master's degree to do our home study. The legal requirements had changed since Micah's adoption, and a bachelor's degree was no longer sufficient. More education meant a higher fee.

All these financial concerns were stressful, but more stressful was the underlying fear that something would happen to thwart the adoption. When Micah was born, we had no contact with his birth mother. Though I didn't really breathe freely until Judge Weckel signed his adoption papers, his birth mother was only a shadowy threat. Anita was a fleshed-out person with whom we had corresponded. I had information about her life, her expectations, her humanity. In addition, now I understood the fiercely protective dimension of motherhood. Before Micah's adoption was final, I had planned to take him and run if anyone tried to remove him from our home—simple enough when the anyone was unknown. To be honest with myself, sometimes I was afraid God would require us to go through these months of anticipation and then, for reasons of His own, strip it away. I had experienced this before. I knew all the pain had been necessary to create our little family, and I knew the pain was assuaged by seeing God's faithfulness and grace. But I still feared His sovereign right to act as He saw fit.

And so I constantly brought my fears back to Him.

I pick up the cross-stitching. I lay tiny Xs into fabric. I remind myself, over and over, "All things, all things, all things…"

CHAPTER 21

The Father's Laugh

> Our mouths were filled with laughter, our tongues with songs of joy. Then it was said among the nations, "The LORD has done great things for them." The LORD has done great things for us, and we are filled with joy.
>
> —Psalm 126:2–3

"My secretary, Cathy, has just handed me a note. Your baby is here! And it's a girl!" The surprise in Pat Neustrom's voice was evident. We had all assumed we would be parents of a boy. The sonogram was wrong.

"A girl? A girl! A girl!" I couldn't stop repeating it. I shifted the phone to my shoulder and wrote "It's a girl!" on my notepad. Debbie Pica, my coworker, looked at the note, gasped, and mouthed, "A girl!"

With difficulty, I tuned back into Pat's words. "Seven pounds, six ounces, twenty inches long, born at 11:58 this morning, and a girl." I could hear the laughter in the background. "Anita wants to meet you and Donnie in person. Can you drive to Hutchinson tomorrow?"

"Let me call him, and I'll get right back with you."

Donnie's reaction was exactly the same: "A girl? A girl! What? A girl? But we don't have a girl's name picked out!"

I laughed and said, "Glory, hallelujah! A girl! We will have one of each!" And then the flash of inspiration: "How about Gloria?" Gloria was a name I would never have thought of, but it seemed so appropriate. Donnie reflected a moment.

"Gloria…Gloria. I like it!"

"What if I send flowers to Anita? And she wants to meet us." I refused to allow the niggling fear to suppress the joy. Still the thought surfaced…what if she doesn't approve of us?

"Yes," I completed my phone order. "A dozen roses. The card should read: 'Her name is Gloria.'" I hung up and tried not to worry about meeting Anita. What should I wear? What would she think? I was on a roller coaster of emotion—amazed that this boy was a girl, overwhelming gratitude toward Anita for her selfless gift, and guilt. This was the most surprising emotion of all. Guilt. The feeling that I was depriving a new mother of her child.

The drive to Hutchinson was a blur. An hour away, we had time to discuss a middle name for Gloria. By the time we arrived, we had settled on Rose, for the Rose of Sharon, one of the names of Jesus in scripture.

The hospital room door was slightly ajar. The voice responding to our knock was quiet. Anita was standing by the window of her room when we entered, dressed in a robe and slippers. He first words were "She will be taller than both of you." Donnie and I looked at each other. Anita was attractive, though she looked tired. She examined us closely. "Thank you for the roses. I like the name you've chosen. Gloria."

As I look back at this meeting, I have a jumble of memories. I can't remember what we talked about in detail. I know Anita told us that Gloria's birth father was tall. I remember that she seemed resigned. I remember that I felt sad for her and my guilt was intensifying. She adjured us to tell Gloria that her decision toward adoption was not because she was a mixed-race baby. I remember her words as we left the hospital room: "You had better take good care of her!"

Our next stop was the nursery, where we met our daughter. The nurses had written *Angel* on her name card, and yes, she looked like an angel to us. We held and fed her and, reluctantly, left to go home. We had people to call and a certain little three-year-old boy to tell.

Micah was cuddled in my lap as I said, "She's very, very little. She can't walk or talk yet, but she will when she grows bigger. She can't play with toys yet, but if you touch her hand with your finger, she will hold it."

Micah looked solemnly from my face to Donnie's. "Is she brown?"

I smiled. "Yes, she's as brown as you. Tomorrow you can go with us to get her from the hospital and bring her home."

"What is her name?"

"Her name is Gloria Rose Mattison."

"Can she sleep in my room?"

"At first she will sleep in a basket in our room so she won't wake you up when she's hungry, but later she can sleep in a crib in your room." We looked at one another. Our plan of having two boys share a room was not going to happen. "When she gets bigger, we will figure out a room for her."

"Can Aunt Bonnie come too?"

"Yes, Aunt Bonnie will stay downstairs with you while we go upstairs in the elevator to get her. They don't let children come into the baby area."

It was a convoy that traveled to Hutchinson the next day. Donnie's mother rode in my mother's Honda sedan, and Bonnie sat in our back seat next to Micah. The weather was unbelievably warm for April. The forecast was that we would hit eighty degrees. That would be a conservative estimate.

Inside the hospital lobby, my sister took charge of Micah, leading him toward the gift shop. By the time we returned from the nursery, he would be sporting a new T-shirt proclaiming "I'm the Big Brother."

Pat, the attorney, met us on the OB floor with the final paperwork. Over his shoulder, I could see an open elevator door and, inside, a stainless-steel cart bore a huge bouquet of red roses. Behind that, a wheelchair transported a patient in street clothes. As the elevator door slid shut, I realized it was Anita, leaving. I breathed a silent prayer for her, that her journey home from the hospital without a baby would not be unbearable. Thankfulness washed over me— thankfulness for Anita's selflessness and for the Father's mercy.

Pat went over the details. We would have to pay the hospital before Gloria could go home with us, as well as the obstetrician who delivered her. Once again, the Father had performed a miracle of provision for us: the mobile home Donnie and his dad had been working on had sold. The money would cover the hospital bill. As he discussed the paperwork with us, he told us we couldn't leave the hospital with Gloria until the adoption papers were filed in Saline county. Gloria's two new grandmothers, Donnie's mother and mine, volunteered to leave right away and drive back to Salina to the court-house. We would wait for the court to fax the certified copy back to us. While we waited, Donnie paid the hospital bill, and I rocked my new daughter and fed her. She nestled in my arms, solemnly watching my face. "You are beautiful, little one. You are glorious. You are Gloria and you are perfect." Her dark eyes began to close, the milk dribbling from the corner of her mouth. I smoothed her curls and raised the warm bundle of her to my shoulder, amazed.

My mother must have driven like Mario Andretti to get back to the courthouse in Salina so fast. Within an hour, we were meeting Bonnie and Micah back in the hospital lobby with his new sister.

Micah remembered what I had told him: "If you touch her hand with your finger, she will hold it." He extended his index fin-ger to her tiny fist, and sure enough, she closed her hand around it. Micah smiled up at us and then down at his new sister.

"Rosie. My baby, Rosie. Don't you love my baby, Mama? Don't you love my baby, Daddy? Don't you love my baby, Aunt Bonnie?"

Donnie and I exchanged glances. Before that moment, it hadn't occurred to us that choosing Rose as Gloria's middle name was also a fulfillment of Micah's prayer for a brown baby sister named Rosie. At that moment, I knew our Father was laughing with us. He gave us a boy that was really a girl, and from this moment she would be called Rosie. I swallowed the lump in my throat and smiled at my son.

"Mama, she's kinda pink."

"Don't worry, son. She'll brown up."

MY PRAYER FOR YOU

Abba, Great Redeemer,

Abba, I have written this out of obedience. You have taught me that You are Faithful and True and You are the Author and the Finisher. You, who did not withhold Your Only Son, but freely gave Him for us all, how much more, then, will you freely give us all things? There is nothing You cannot do. May this story, above all, be to the praise of the glory of Your grace. For all that read this account, I pray, Father, that they will see Your hand at work and know that You are there and that You redeem all things.

I pray for the barren and the broken, that this story of barrenness and brokenness will facilitate healing for them.

I pray, Father, for those who read this and are in loveless marriages, that they may know that Blood of the Lamb is for them, so that they can forgive and be forgiven.

I pray, Father, for those who have borne children and released them to be adopted by other parents. Abba, comfort them when they grieve. Show them You, too, gave Your Son.

I pray, Father, for those who are adopted and may struggle with rejection or feelings of betrayal. I pray You will show Yourself as the Spirit of Adoption, and they will know You, the Father Who sets the solitary in families.

I pray, Father, for those who are not living the life they wanted or dreamed of. You, Redeemer of all, give silver in the place of iron and for brass You give gold.

In the mighty name of Jesus,
Amen.

ABOUT THE AUTHOR

Lola Mattison lives and works with her husband as a farmer in central Kansas. She enjoys travel, gardening, and building relationships. Lola gleans satisfaction from the rhythms of seasonal tasks. Her philosophy of life can be summed up thus: "Everything must be fed, watered, or cleaned."

CPSIA information can be obtained
at www.ICGtesting.com
Printed in the USA
LVHW052313210520
656048LV00003B/292